The Fuel Savers

A Kit of Solar Ideas for Your Home, Apartment, or Business

EDITED BY BRUCE N. ANDERSON

Distributed to the trade by: Publishers Group West
1-800-365-3453

The authors of the original *Fuel Savers* in 1978 were Dan Scully, Bruce Anderson, and Don Prowler. Bruce was President at that time of Total Environmental Action, Inc., a research, design, consulting and education firm then based in Harrisville, New Hampshire. Dan was Senior Architect. Don Prowler, an architect, lectured at the University of Pennsylvania Graduate School of Architecture in Philadelphia, where he is now an assistant professor. Both Dan and Don now have their own architecture practices, Dan in Peterborough, NH and Don in Philadelphia.

Special thanks to Charles Corcoran, Director, Housing and Community Development for NORWESCAP, who conceived and made possible the original report on which the first edition of *The Fuel Savers* was based.

Special thanks also to Andy Merriell, on whose original illustrations those in this book are based.

Publisher: Jack Howell
Cover Design & Electronic Publishing: Kathleen M. Gadway
Production Assistance: Dave Souza

ISBN 0-9629069-0-5

2   3   4   5   6   7   8   9   10   11   12

NOTE: The appearance of an idea in *The Fuel Savers* does not indicate that owners of patents and copyrights have granted any release to users of this book.

This is an IEG Book from International Environment Group, Inc, 71 Sargent Camp Rd, Peterborough, NH 03458.

One-half of all of the royalties on this book are being contributed to the Dr. John and Barbara Yellott Scholarship Fund of the American Solar Energy Society, Boulder, Colorado. Dr. Yellott was one of the world's foremost solar pioneers and friends of the earth. The other half of royalties are being contributed to the National Foundation on Poverty and the Environment, Peterborough, NH, addressing the relationship between problems of the environment and poverty.

Individual copies: $4.95 plus $1.50 postage and handling. Discounts available for quantity orders.

Morning Sun Press books are available at quantity discounts when used to promote products or services. For information please write to Premium Marketing Department, Morning Sun Press, P.O. Box 413, Lafayette, CA 94549 (415) 932-1383 FAX (415) 934-8277.

Praise for The Fuel Savers

"Solar energy will surely be the key to a safer future, and everyone can start entering the future now, thanks to this user-friendly, helpful book."

Paul R. Ehrlich
author of THE POPULATION BOMB
and Bing Professor of Population Studies, Stanford University

"This practical, affordable little book is a must for anyone who wants solar ideas, complete with their payback ratios, to help in determining what solar projects, if any, are feasible for ones home and climate."

Janet Groene
Contributing Editor, Homeowner Magazine

"In only 83 pages Anderson collects the basics of how consumers can reduce reliance upon fossil fuels... a comprehensive review of systems for home owners."

The Bookwatch
The Midwest Book Review

"Homeowners should be able to utilize THE FUEL SAVERS as a useful primer if they are considering solar to complement energy efficiency upgrades for their homes."

Winston K. Ashizawa
Director, Energy Efficiency, Sacramento Municipal Utility District

"THE FUEL SAVERS is an entertaining, yet tremendously educational look at ways to save energy and money from the simplest do-it-yourself ideas to choosing a complex professional system."

George Kiskaddon
Builders Booksource, Berkeley, CA

"Well written and easy to understand - THE FUEL SAVERS could be of great benefit to homeowners in reducing energy bills."

James A. Smith
Energy Program Manager, Energy and Home Environment Department
National Association of Home Builders

Foreword

Even if you are not buying or building a new house, there are still many ways to harness solar energy and slash skyrocketing fuel bills. A number of these solar heating projects are within the range of skills of the average person who is handy around the house.

The sun shines on us all, old and young, rich and poor alike. Its energy is plentiful, harmless and free, so it makes good sense to use it. Plus, by using solar energy you will not only reduce your fuel bills but help solve one of the most urgent problems of our time — environment degradation. The most important thing we can do to help the environment is to change the way we use energy. This means kicking the fossil fuel (oil, gas and coal) habit and switching to the only long term clean source — the sun.

You've probably heard that using solar energy to help heat your house is relatively simple. For example, the best solar collector in the world is a south-facing window. You've probably also heard that the cost of using solar energy is still high. This is often true. However, you can cut costs considerably by taking things into your own hands — by doing much of the work yourself.

With this in mind, *The Fuel Savers* describes solar energy systems that can be constructed at moderate costs and as do-it-yourself projects. These systems are simply constructed, durable and straightforward in operation so that they perform well over long periods of time. Most can be built onto a wide range of existing buildings. Even though this book addresses the homeowner and many references are made to "your home," many of the ideas work just as well in apartment buildings, offices and industrial buildings.

The Fuel Savers does not include pre-engineered and manufactured products, or solar system components which use expensive parts such as heat pumps, metal tube-in-plate absorber plates, heat exchangers of the sophisticated variety used by engineers, and other store-bought solar heating components. Instead, this book includes a variety of ways to use solar energy, ranging from very simple devices to fairly complex systems. You can decide which ideas best suit your site, your house, your know-how and your pocketbook. Remember that these are suggestions, not blueprints. Before you start many of the projects you should do further reading. There is a complete list of publications in the appendix

We hope this kit of ideas will also help you branch out, perhaps even design your own device. The principles involved in solar energy are identical for new and old construction. And there is ample room for ingenuity in applying these principles to your specific problems.

Energy Conservation

The most cost-effective and sensible approach to reducing your fuel bills and helping the environment is energy conservation. Using solar energy is usually more expensive than conservation and should come as the next step after you've done everything possible to use energy more efficiently.

The two most important things to do to conserve energy are to lower your thermostat and weatherize your home. The first method is the more direct. You control the rate of usage with the thermostat. Lower temperatures in the house mean less fuel consumed. It's that simple. Many people (the British are famous for it) can be quite comfortable at temperatures below 68 degrees — they save both money and energy. If you're uncomfortable at those temperatures, insulate your body with a sweater rather than raise the thermostat. It also makes good sense to lower the temperature at least 5 degrees at night. It's not true that you burn more fuel reheating the house in the morning than you saved overnight. Look for clock thermostats in your local home center to automatically lower and raise the termperatuare of your house. And remember, learning to live with a higher temperature during the summer reduces air conditioning bills.

WEATHERIZATION

Weatherization is central to any program of energy conservation. This book cannot completely cover weatherization. It is important, however, to learn some of the most important measures which you can use to weatherize your home. A brief approach to weatherization is outlined below and may be supplemented by other sources (see *Appendix*).

The illustration below shows by percentage the amount of heat loss in three houses of the same size and shape, but with differing qualities of insulation. The poorly insulated house has 100 percent heat loss, the moderately insulated house has 60 percent heat loss, and the well insulated house has only 25 percent heat loss. Heat loss occurs in two ways: infiltration and conduction.

INFILTRATION

In all the houses, much of the heat is lost through cracks and openings; cold air leaks in and replaces expensive, heated air. This type of heat loss is called "infiltration."

To combat infiltration, first locate the leak and use caulk to seal any large, obvious holes in windows, foundations, roofs, etc. Next, recaulk smaller cracks around windows and door frames. You can hold a lighted candle near windows and other suspected openings to locate leaks.

Next, weatherstrip your windows and doors. This seals the small openings at the bottom, top and sides of doors and windows. Don't skimp on the cost of weatherstripping (available at hardware stores); the more expensive will usually remain tighter longer and save more energy.

After you caulk and weatherstrip windows and doors, the most productive step is to add another layer of glass, such as storm windows. This can save from ⅓–½ of the heat that infiltration loses through your window. This is covered further on page 10.

If you feel you have made your house so tight that the air seems no longer to be as fresh as you'd like, you need to look for an air-to-air heat exchanger. This uses outgoing exhaust air to heat incoming replacement air, saving a considerable amount of money.

CONDUCTION

Comparing losses in the three houses, the poorly insulated house loses the most heat through conduction. In the best house, conduction losses are dramatically reduced. Conduction occurs when heat passes through building materials, such as wood and plasterboard, directly to the cold outdoors. The best way to reduce conduction heat loss is to insulate. Insulating materials slow the heat flow through walls, ceilings or other surfaces. Attics, easily accessible and one of the greatest sources of conductive heat loss, should be well insulated with at least 10 inches of mineral wool insulation or its thermal equivalent. When possible, use one of the many available methods to insulate exterior walls (if they are not already well-insulated). Use rigid board insulations on interior surfaces and then cover with gypsum wallboard or applied to exterior surfaces if you add new siding at the same time. Or insulation can be blown into walls through small holes cut in the siding and then resealed. Flammable insulation when improperly used can be a fire hazard, so be careful! Avoid

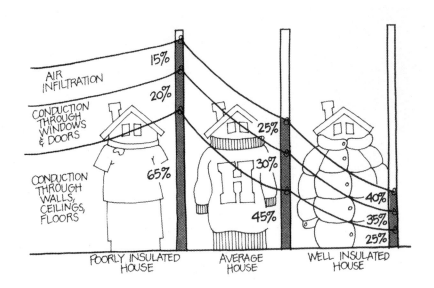

AIR INFILTRATION

CONDUCTION THROUGH WINDOWS & DOORS

CONDUCTION THROUGH WALLS, CEILINGS, FLOORS

15%
20%
65%

25%
30%
45%

40%
35%
25%

POORLY INSULATED HOUSE

AVERAGE HOUSE

WELL INSULATED HOUSE

polyurethane foam because of the CFCs they contain that damage the earth's ozone layer. Also, note that ureaformaldehyde foam has been banned because of its health affects. Fiberglass and cellulose fiber are the safest. Ask your local fire officials if you have a question.

You should also make sure that your furnace works properly — clean it periodically so that you receive the most energy from your fuel. Also consider heating only the areas of your home which you use most in the winter.

Insulation is usually thought of as an important part of walls, floors and ceilings, but people are realizing that insulating over window areas is also very important. Although windows take up only a small percentage of the building surface, the illustration shows that conductive heat loss through windows is considerable. So windows are an important source of heat loss — but they are also one of the most important types of solar collectors. In the text you will find a number of ways of dealing with this two-sided nature of windows.

Solar Energy

ORIENTATION

To "orient" means to correctly position in relation to the environment. Ideally, a solar device should face due south. However, even devices that cannot face exactly south can still be effective. From the illustration, we can see how much sunshine is lost for vertical wall surfaces located at latitude 40 degrees north facing orientations other than true south. A vertical wall surface oriented as much as 30 degrees east or west of due south will still receive 90 percent of the maximum solar radiation striking a south-facing wall. Even with a 45 degree deviation from due south, a vertical collector can still catch about 72 percent of the maximum possible radiation striking a south-facing wall. These figures apply to the winter heating season when collecting sunshine is most important. Even walls facing as far as 60 degrees from due south can collect substantial amounts of solar energy.

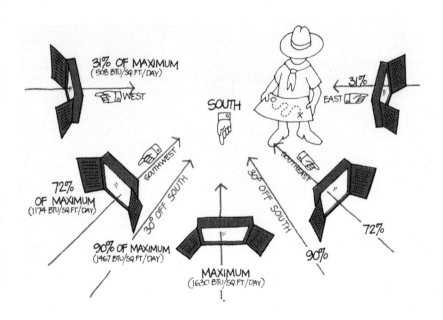

TILT

Like the orientation, the tilt of the collecting surface affects how much solar energy can be gathered. A tilt angle equal to your latitude plus 15 degrees from the horizontal collects the most solar energy. For example, at a latitude of 40 degrees, the optimum would be 55 degrees.

For vertical surfaces, performance can be greatly increased by the presence of a reflecting surface such as snow. Therefore, if you are unable to place your collecting surface at an angle, reflection onto the vertical collector helps you collect the available energy. In fact, a vertical collecting surface, combined with horizontal reflection can sometimes collect more energy than a surface tilted to the "ideal."

The accompanying figures demonstrate that tilts as much as 20 degrees to 30 degrees from optimum can still intercept over 90 percent of the available daily insolation (solar radiation, ie sunlight) per unit area. From a practical viewpoint, this suggests a considerable leeway. You may have many reasons to build or use a surface with less than optimum tilt or orientation. If the device is part of or attached to an existing building, you must use the surfaces you already have. A free-standing device can be more flexibly placed, but other things may interfere — trees, neighbors' houses, even hills may block the ideal orientation. Or it may look too obtrusive to have a large solar device sitting at an odd angle. As our figures demonstrate, if the collecting surface cannot tilt or face in the "ideal" direction, the decrease in solar collection need not be excessive. Your own good judgment will guide you in choosing the best angles for particular situations.

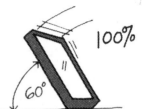

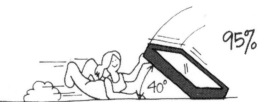

A Kit Of Ideas

The ideas in this book vary widely in complexity and cost. Some projects may cost little or nothing, if you already have the supplies on hand. Others may amount to substantial investments. Within each section of the book there is a progression from simple projects to more complex ones. Cost-effectiveness usually parallels that progression. The simpler ideas are often more cost-effective. The complicated ones may offer the same fuel savings yet cost a great deal more.

In order to give you an idea of the relative merits of each idea from the point of view of energy saved per dollar spent, the last items in the discussion of each idea are *Materials Costs, Fuel Reduction,* and *Cost-Effectiveness.* The costs are those for the necessary materials, assuming you have to buy most of them. No cost for labor is included as most of the projects are feasible for the do-it-yourselfer. The fuel reduction is given as oil or electrical savings. Your actual saving will depend on the present and future fuel cost.

If you use electricity, 30 kilowatt-hours (kWh) of electric power is the equivalent of about one gallon of oil heat, burned at a furnace efficiency of 75 percent. Thus, if your electric company charges $.10 per kWh, the equivalent of one gallon of oil would cost you $3.00. To find your local equivalent price of electricity, multiply the rate per kilowatt-hour by 30.

As for natural gas, 125 cubic feet is the equivalent of one gallon of oil. To get the equivalent cost of the natural gas, multiply the charge for 100 cubic feet (1 ccf) by $1.25. If you use bottled gas which sells by the pound, use 4.5 pounds of gas as the equivalent of one gallon of oil. The equivalent cost of the bottled gas can be figured if you multiply the price per pound by 4.5. You may want to include some estimate of price inflation in your calculations of energy saving over the years.

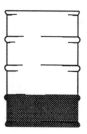 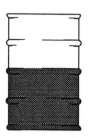 

At the end of each discussion is an oil barrel diagram, which shows the relative cost-effectiveness of each idea presented. **The amount of oil left in the barrel represents the amount of energy saved relative to the amount of money spent.** Therefore, a high level indicates that not much money need be spent to save a lot of energy. A low level indicates that not much energy is saved for the amount of money spent. The cost-effectiveness ratings on a scale of 1–20 correspond to the levels in the barrel.

The ideas are presented schematically, with discussions of advantages, disadvantages and variations. Construction details are not given because there are so few "typical" situations in retrofitting. The *Appendix* will help you find additional detailed information.

Additional Glazing

Most windows save energy in two ways. They admit sunlight (solar energy), which turns to heat, and they reduce the flow of outgoing heat by blocking the movement of heat. When you add a second or third layer of glazing, such as storm windows or a layer of plastic, you reduce the transparency of the window, but by a much, much larger factor you increase the insulating value of the window by creating dead air spaces and forming another barrier to air leakage through the window. In other words, with each additional layer, less heat moves from your warm room to the cold outdoors. A third layer will save almost twice as much energy as adding just a second layer.

Each layer should be installed tightly to keep out drafts. Second and third layers of transparent materials can be made easily by stretching plastic over a light frame. Weatherstrip or caulk for air-tightness. Leave small "weep holes" at the bottom of the storm window so that any inside condensation can drain away.

The most permanent solution is to use glass in wooden or metal frames that can remain in place year round or, alternatively, removed, stored and reused for years. You may be able to buy or scrounge second-hand storm windows that fit. If not, new ones are usually a worthwhile investment.

VARIATIONS
• An even cheaper method is to tack or staple plastic film directly to the window frame. This, however, is neither durable nor attractive.

WHERE THIS WORKS
This solution can (and should) be applied to all windows. If you can't do them all at once, do the north windows first and work your way around the west and east sides to the south side. During the winter in the Northern Hemisphere, the sun almost never shines through northern windows. Therefore, north-facing windows provide no solar gain and actually lose significant amounts of heat. Insulate them first!

ADVANTAGES
• Additional glazing is relatively cheap and saves lots of energy.
• It's easy to install and applicable to all window types and locations.
• It insulates the area of greatest heat loss in your house while allowing sunlight to shine in.

DISADVANTAGES
• You may have to remove additional glazing in the spring and re-install it in the fall.

STORM WINDOW

PLASTIC ON WOOD FRAME

- It may interfere with the opening of the window for ventilation or for emergency exit.
- A plastic glazing may blur the view.

ECONOMICS

Materials Costs: The materials for adding a second or third layer can cost from $.25, if you scrounge, up to $10.00 per square foot for custom-made, store-bought units. If you make them yourself, the maximum cost will probably be $1.50 per square foot. For a 10-square-foot window, the cost will be between $2.50 to $15.00.

Fuel Reduction: Putting a second layer over a square foot of window can save from ⅓ to 1 gallon of fuel oil per heating season. A 10-square-foot window will save from 3 to 10 gallons per winter. Adding both a second and a third layer will save somewhat less than twice that amount.

Cost-effectiveness: On the 1–20 scale, this suggestion earns a rating of 18–20.

Flexible Insulating Curtains

Windows can be the most efficient solar collectors. Yet once solar energy enters and heats the room, the easiest way to lose heat is back through these same windows. One way to reduce this heat loss is to cover windows with insulating curtains when the sun has stopped shining.

Make sure the curtains fit tightly to eliminate the movement of warm room air between the cold window surface and the closed curtain. Attach the curtain securely at the top, sides and bottom. A fixed valance (see illustration) is the best way to get a snug fit across the top. Make sure that you weight the bottom of the curtain or in some way make it fairly airtight along the sill to keep warm air from mixing with the cold air behind the curtain.

VARIATIONS
- Curtains can be constructed to roll up and be secured at the top of the window during the sunshine hours. Velcro strips along the sides will keep the curtains tight and draft-free at night.
- Curtains made of heavy quilts, multi-layered fabrics, or quarter-inch flexible foam insulation covered with your choice of fabric will prevent excessive heat loss.
- One of the best insulating curtains uses several layers of material which traps air between each layer.

WHERE THIS WORKS
Insulating curtains can be used in a wonderful variety of situations. Any window (with some room around the edge) is a prime target for insulating curtains. To maximize the benefit from your curtain, make sure you first seal any cracks or leaks in the existing window and its frame.

ADVANTAGES
- An insulating curtain is the easiest way to change an energy-collecting daytime window into an energy-conserving nighttime window.
- Insulating curtains are simple and inexpensive; they offer significant fuel savings for anyone willing to spend the time.
- Because it is a simple indoor device, your insulating curtain should have a long lifetime — reducing your fuel bill all the while.

DISADVANTAGES
- You must be willing to open and close your curtains every day to reap maximum benefits. If you get lazy you won't save as much energy (and money) as you could.
- When open, the curtain takes up wall space. In some cases there may not be enough wall space around your window for the curtain.

VALANCE

FASTENED AT SIDES

WEIGHTED AT BOTTOM

- A flexible curtain will not be as tight or as well insulated as a rigid shutter (see next section) yet could cost as much or more.

ECONOMICS

Materials Costs: The materials can cost from $1.00 to $3.00 for each square foot of your curtain. Therefore, it will cost from $10.00 to $30.00 for a 10-square-foot window. If you use fancy materials this figure could be higher. Many commercial models are available, too.

Fuel Reduction: For each square foot of window-surface covered each night with a flexible insulating curtain, the savings is from ⅓–½ gallon of fuel oil each heating season. A 10-square-foot curtain (an average window size) will save from 1–5 gallons per year.

Cost-effectiveness: On the 1–20 scale, this suggestion earns a rating of 14–16.

Rigid Insulating Shutters

Insulating shutters are a more effective alternative to cloth insulating curtains for reducing heat loss through your windows at night. You can make a simple insulating shutter from 2 inches of insulation (the more the better) surrounded by a wooden frame and mounted to the wall with hinges.

Besides insulating a window at night, a tight-fitting shutter will also cut down on cold air leaking into the house around the window's edges. Weatherstripping along the edge of the shutter will help seal it more tightly.

The biggest design issue is where the shutter will go when it's not covering the window. This might vary from room to room. See *Variations*. For the money, this is a good energy saver.

VARIATIONS

You can use a wide variety of materials and thicknesses. The easiest to make are 1 and 2 inch thick boards of rigid insulation; the greater the thickness, the greater the energy-savings. Instead of rigid foam plastics, fiberglass or other insulating materials can be used.

- Shutters can be mounted on sliding tracks across windows, hinged up, down or sideways.
- The hardware used to support the shutters can range from continuous cloth hinges to fancy hardwood frames with piano hinges.
- Weatherstrip along the edges and place latches at top and bottom to pull the shutter snug with the window frame. For lightweight shutters, you can use magnetic catches, as in the illustration.

WHERE THIS WORKS

These inside insulating shutters are most appropriate in cold, freezing climates where snow and ice would accumulate on outside mounted shutters.

ADVANTAGES

- A good shutter provides effective insulation for the windows — where it's needed most.
- Shutters are easy to make and operate, requiring no fancy tools or mechanisms.
- A tight-fitting shutter greatly reduces cold air drafts around windows, making the house considerably more comfortable.

DISADVANTAGES

- One problem is condensation. Since the glass is on the cold side of an indoor shutter, water vapor which works its way from the inside of the

house out through the shutters will condense on the glass and wet the framing around the window. Due to the tighter (but not perfect) seal around the shutter, the problem can be more severe for shutters than curtains.

- Some plastic foam boards are fire hazards and may produce toxic gases when ignited. Therefore, they are safest when covered with a fire-proof material. Check with local fire code officials for their recommendations. Avoid CFC-loaded rigid insulations.
- In the open position, or when removed, the shutter takes up space.

ECONOMICS

Materials Costs: There are a variety of ways to build a shutter, but costs should range from $1.20 to $4.50 per square foot. A 10-square-foot shutter would, therefore, cost between $12.50 and $45.00.

Fuel Reduction: If used every night, an insulating shutter of about 10 square feet (an average window size) will save you up to 7½ gallons of oil heat every winter.

Cost-effectiveness: On the 1–20 scale, this suggestion earns a rating of 16–18.

Outside Shutters

An outdoor insulating shutter hinges on the outside of your house. It swings open during the day to allow sunlight through the window; at night, the shutter closes to trap the heat inside. For maximum insulating effectiveness, the shutter should close snugly. In summer, when the house overheats, the shutters can be closed or partly closed to keep sunlight out. You needn't open every window to close the shutters. Go outside to do it, or devise a remote-control method of closing.

By lining the inside of the shutters with a reflective material, you can use the open shutters as reflectors, directing more heat-producing sunshine into the house. A shiny foil also reflects heat back into the house when the shutters are closed. On east and west facing walls, a reflecting and insulating shutter can bounce southern light directly into the room when direct sunshine is not normally available. Be sure to design a shutter that will endure bad weather, wind, or snow falling off the roof.

VARIATIONS
- Your outside insulating shutters can hinge from the sides as shown or from the top and/or bottom of the window. If on the south side, you can also use them as reflectors and shutters. Hinging them on the top and bottom is most effective.
- Top hinging shutters can be used as summer awnings.
- Instead of using a hinge, your shutter could slide on a track or be completely removed and stored during the day.

WHERE THIS WORKS
This shutter will be effective on any window. Whenever a window is in shade, shuttering it will save energy.

ADVANTAGES
- Exterior shutters do not have the condensation problems that sometimes plague interior shutters.
- This is a simple, effective device which the average weekend carpenter can easily construct.

DISADVANTAGES
- The biggest disadvantage is having to operate the shutters — even during the coldest and snowiest days. Yet it is precisely on these days, when you don't want to go outside to close your shutters, that they do the most good and save you the most money.
- Exposure to the outdoors increases wear and tear on the materials, paint and hardware.

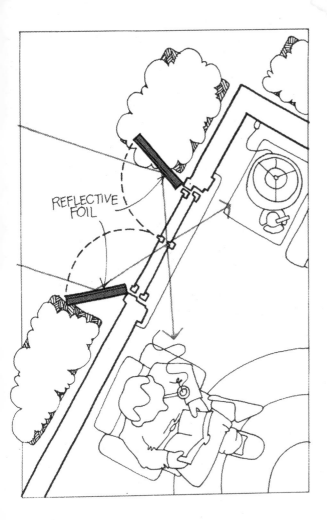

REFLECTIVE FOIL

- Ice and snow can impair operation.

ECONOMICS

Materials Costs: Materials can cost from $2.50 to $6.50 for each square foot of shutter. A 10-square-foot shutter would thus cost from $25.00 to $65.00. Add up to $.50 per square foot for a reflecting surface.

Fuel Reduction: For each square foot of window surface covered each night with an outside insulating shutter, you should be able to save ⅕ to ¾ gallon of oil per season. A 10-square-foot shutter will save 2 to 7½ gallons a year. If your shutter acts as a reflector as well, you can increase savings by as much as 20 percent.

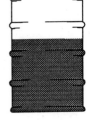

Cost-effectiveness: On the 1–20 scale. this suggestion earns a rating of 12–14.

Adding New Windows

Consider adding a window to the south wall of your house. During the winter a double-glazed southerly window gains more heat energy from the sun than it loses back to the cold outside. Be sure to add a storm window or use double or triple glass or new "low-emissivity" (low-e) glazings. Install it tightly to prevent air from leaking around the frame and into the house. Now insulate your window at night with an insulating curtain or movable insulation (such as a shutter) and you have one of the best solar collectors possible!

Two things to remember: First, be careful when cutting through walls of your house. Consult with a contractor or architect first to avoid undue damage. Secondly, when the window is finished, keep the curtains open and let the sun shine in! If you want to prevent fading of your upholstery, move the furniture and open the drapes!

VARIATIONS
- Your new window can be either fixed or movable. Fixed glass allows less cold air to sneak in but can't be opened for ventilation.
- Windows come in many sizes and types, from colonial double-hung to bay windows and sliding glass doors.
- Skylights are windows, too. Because hot air rises, it is especially important that skylights have insulating shutters.

WHERE THIS WORKS
This works almost anywhere on the south side of your building. Just don't cut out wall structure that's supporting your building, and be careful not to cut into electrical wiring or plumbing.

ADVANTAGES
- The advantages of windows are obvious — more sun for your plants, a better view of the world...

DISADVANTAGES
- It is possible to get excessive heat, especially in the summer, if too much of the south wall is glass. You may have to add materials (see *Thermal Mass*) to absorb this excess heat.
- New windows may not add to the appearance of your house.

ECONOMICS
Materials Costs: A regular sized window (about 10 square feet) will cost about $100 to $300 plus trim materials, reframing and labor. Bigger win-

dows cost more. Tight, well weatherstripped windows do too, but keeping out cold air infiltration is worth the extra expense.

Fuel Reduction: Each square foot of window area can save you from ½ to 1 gallon of oil per heating season. A 10-square-foot window will save from 5–10 gallons a winter.

Cost-effectiveness: On the 1–20 scale, this suggestion earns a rating of 9-12.

Awnings

Wherever summer cooling is a major concern, use shading devices to block the intense summer sun from your south windows, from all passive solar heating devices, and from your sunroom or sunspace. A shade on the outside of your house does the job better than interior shades because it keeps the sun off the window altogether. Interior shades let the sun in first and are less effective at reducing cooling bills.

The four sides of your house have different shading needs. The east and west sides of houses receive two times more sun in summer than in winter. Awnings and overhangs do not work well on the east and west sides of a house because the rising and setting sun beams its light onto the windows at a very low angle. Trellises, plants, shrubs and trees can be used there (see next section). Windows on the north side of your house do not need shading.

On the south side, awnings can be rolled down on April 1 and kept down until October 1. In its fully rolled-out summertime position, the awning shades the window and provides a pleasant light for the room inside without eliminating all natural daylight. Then the awning can be rolled up in winter, leaving the building fully exposed to the heat of the winter sun.

Properly designed, fixed overhangs and awnings can do a good job of blocking out the sun's rays in the summer, and they don't interfere with the sunlight entering your house in the winter when the sun is low in the sky. But the drawback of fixed devices is that they shade a window just as much in March as in September. And in March you will still want to take advantage of the sun's warmth. Adjustable shades are the most efficient because they can be positioned to respond to the sun's changing position in the sky.

VARIATIONS
• Awnings can be made of aluminum or canvas.
• Fixed overhangs may be effective on the south side of your house.

ADVANTAGES
• An adjustable awning provides you with just the amount of sun protection you want at any time of year.
• It is easy to operate — just crank it opened and closed.

DISADVANTAGES
- Because they are outside and exposed to wind, weather, and nesting animals, awnings do not have a long lifetime.

ECONOMICS
Materials Costs: Awnings for an average window can range from $20.00 to $100, depending on the material and the design.

Fuel Reduction: shaded east or west windows can save about $6.00 per window each year by reducing the cooling load. If they shade south-facing windows, the annual cooling load reduction will amount to a savings of $2.00 to $3.00 per window.

Cost Savings: On a scale of 1–20, this suggestion rates a 10–12.

Trellises and Vegetation

Fortunately, when Mother Nature gave us the sun, she also gave us plants that can be used to shade our homes in the summer. In the summer, bushes, small trees, and trellises on the east and west sides of the house are the best solution for blocking out the low-angled light of the morning and afternoon sun. And when you want that solar heat in the winter, the leaves have dropped off, letting the sun's rays through. In ideal situations, proper use of vegetation can reduce the summer cooling load to 20–25 percent of what it was.

Leafy trees can shade portions of the roof and walls in the summer, and the air drawn into the house from the shaded areas will be cooler. Remember a tree's bare trunk and branches can significantly shade south-facing collectors and windows in the winter, decreasing their ability to collect solar energy.

Vines growing up on stakes or on an overhead trellis will also do an excellent shading job. A trellis is simple to build, using wire, lumber or even fencing. Just make sure it is tall enough to shade the windows when the sun is highest in the sky. A shaded patio area can be created next to your house by building out from it with an overhead trellis and a wall trellis. Be careful to ensure that the trellis does not block the sun in the winter.

Try planting sunflowers and other tall vegetables that grow quickly on stakes or poles just a few feet from your house. Locating the vegetation a few feet from the house will provide shade without blocking the breeze. Also, plants release large amounts of moisture and so locating them too close to the house can make the air uncomfortably humid.

VARIATIONS
- You can grow vines over porches to shade outdoor spaces and wall areas
- If you know the prevailing wind patterns at your house, you can plant shrubbery so that it funnels a breeze into the house.

ADVANTAGES
- Trees, shrubs, vines and plants are alive and beautiful!
- This type of shading is an investment that will last a lifetime.
- If you plant tall-growing vegetables, you can eat your shade at the end of the summer!

DISADVANTAGES
- You need a green thumb!

WIRE TRELLIS

ARBOR

ECONOMICS

Materials Costs: A simple lean-to wire trellis as shown in the illustration will cost about $40.00 for materials, while an arbor built with some framing members and wire could cost as much as $100. The cost of plants is extra.

Fuel Reduction: Annual savings for east and west windows will be around $6.00 per window and for south windows, just over $2.00.

Cost-Effectiveness: On a scale of 1–20, this suggestion rates a 8–10.

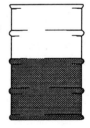

Introduction

The most attractive solar addition you can make to any house is a sunroom, such as a sunspace, greenhouse, or glassed in porch. Handsome looking on the exterior, they create a very pleasant living space inside. While these add-ons are not low-cost ideas, if well built they will increase the value and pleasure of living in your home as well as help cut down on heating costs. To build them, you need a wall (or porch) that faces south (or within 45 degrees of south) and solid skills in house carpentry and installing glass.

The number of designs available for sunspaces, greenhouses, and glassed in porches are as varied as the houses to which they can be added. One important design decision is whether to set the glass in a vertical position or to tilt it. For sunspaces and sunrooms, vertical glass is popular because it allows people enough headroom to easily move about and use the entire space. Vertical glass is also easier to install and has less tendency to overheat a space. For heating purposes, however, glass at an angle of 60 degrees from horizontal lets in more sun.

Glass for greenhouses is usually tilted so that the plants both in front and back can get good amounts of light. A shallow angle of 45 degrees from the horizontal collects more light in spring and fall but the angle of the glass leaves less headroom at the front of the greenhouse. Steeper angles near 60 degrees from the horizontal m aximize winter growth, but compared with 45 degrees glass growth in the Spring would be reduced when the greenhouse may be full of seedlings.

Leaks are often a problem for glass installed at a sloping angle. Before you build, talk to people who have experience and get their advice. There are a number of leak-proof designs. Books and how-to plans listed in the *Appendix* will also give you tips for dealing with this problem.

Thermal mass (heavy material, such as brick, concrete or water) is used to store heat in a greenhouse for nighttime and to slow down the rapid temperature rise during the day. Storage materials don't have to take up space inside a greenhouse; they can be placed under the growing beds or under shelves. Just expose a large surface area of thermal mass to the sun. Plastic gallon jugs filled with water can be piled anywhere. Because they're inexpensive, second-hand 55 gallon drums are often used. But they do take up a lot of space, are difficult to move when full and can rust after a few years. In a larger greenhouse, build planting beds of concrete-filled blocks; you can finish them with stucco to make them look better. A gravel floor or concrete slab will store some heat. So will a back wall made of brick. And soil itself, particularly when it's wet, does an excellent job of holding a lot of heat and releasing it slowly.

The amount of thermal mass you need depends on why you want the greenhouse. If the greenhouse is for heating first and growing second, the amount of mass can be moderate and you can use a large fan to pull air into the house. If growing plants is your first love and house heat your second, then you'll need more thermal mass to maintain the desired temperatures. For help in deciding how much mass you need, see *Appendix.*

Be sure to ventilate your greenhouse or sunspace to the outside. The area of these vents should be at least 20 percent of the floor area. At one end of the greenhouse or sunspace, place a low vent facing the prevailing winds. At the other end, place one high up.

Whichever sunroom you choose — sunspace, greenhouse, or glassed in porch — you can't go wrong. Solar add-ons will give you pleasure — and heat — for years to come.

Sunspaces

A sunspace or sunroom can be a pleasant dining area or a playroom for your children. Best of all, it is a good source of heat for your house. The south wall of the sunspace is covered with two layers of glass. This glass can be titled or vertical. Sunlight shining through the glass warms the air inside, which then flows through vents into the main living area of your house. A fan placed in an opening high on the wall is important for moving the hot air into the house. A register placed into the house wall at floor level will allow cooler house air to enter the sunspace and be warmed. To keep the heat inside your house on those days when the temperatures in the sunspace are cool, the wall that separates the two areas needs to be insulated. You will want to enjoy the light from the sunspace. Up to 50 square feet of that wall can be insulating glass. You can build your sunspace right onto an insulated wall that has a door and windows in it.

It can be surprisingly warm inside a sunspace on a cold and sunny winter day. Make sure that no trees or nearby houses will shade the sunspace from 9 a.m. to 3 p.m. during the heating season. In the cooling season try to completely block direct sunlight from the sunspace. The design should include at least two vents to the outdoors so that excess sunspace heat can be released when the house doesn't need it. Vent areas should total 20 percent of the floor area.

VARIATIONS
- The glass can be either vertical or tilted, but preferably tilted.
- The end walls can either be double glazed or closed in and insulated.
- In addition to the door from the house into the sunspace, you may want one connecting to the outdoors too.

ADVANTAGES
- This is an attractive, heat-producing addition to the outside of your home .
- Operating a sunspace takes less owner attention than a greenhouse.
- Because it doesn't need thermal mass, a sunspace costs less that greenhouse.

DISADVANTAGES
- This project is not for an inexperienced builder.
- Care must be taken to avoid overheating in the summer

ECONOMICS

Materials Costs: The materials for a sunspace will range between $25.00 and $40.00 per square foot of floor area, with a 120 square foot sunspace costing $3,000–$4,800. Commercial sunspaces can cost $10,000 or more.

Fuel Reduction: A 120 square foot sunspace can save around $90.00 per year if completely shaded in summer. This is equivalent to 1,600–2,000 kWh of electricity.

Cost Effectiveness: On a scale of 1–20, this suggestion earns a rate of 6–7 .

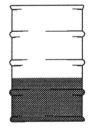

Greenhouses

Attach a greenhouse to the south wall and gather extra solar heat for your house while growing plants and vegetables. This unit is supported by the wall of the house with a door and window, or several windows. The greenhouse glass collects heat from the sun and reduces heat loss from the house when the sun is not shining. To absorb heat, the greenhouse pictured has a dark gravel floor and a concrete door-step. If yours does not have a doorstep you could add some heat-absorbing masonry or containers of water.

Remember, as air warms it rises naturally. When the greenhouse gets too warm, a movable hinged top can be flipped up to ventilate it. You can open or close the door and window of the house to regulate the amount of heat entering from the greenhouse.

Make the frame from wood and cover it with glass. If possible, avoid plastic. It has a short life span, doesn't look good, and is not good for the environment. Keep the amount of wood or other material in the frame to a minimum; too much blocks out the solar energy. Be careful not to place your greenhouse where ice or snow falling off the roof can damage it.

VARIATIONS
You can construct a smaller greenhouse that attaches to any window frame. One kind is the same size as the window, about 12 inches deep. It has two wire mesh shelves to allow the free flow of warmed air. A hinged top or movable center panel on the top provides ventilation.

WHERE THIS WORKS
South-facing walls are much preferred, although southeast and southwest walls are acceptable. East and west walls are exposed to sun only half the day. Be sure there are no large buildings that might shade your greenhouse in the wintertime when the sun is low on the horizon.

ADVANTAGES
- A greenhouse not only provides home heat, but the plants inside provide moisture during dry winter months.
- Larger greenhouses can also provide food. Greenhouses offer an early start for garden seedlings.

DISADVANTAGES
- On cold winter nights you may have to open the window and use home heat to warm the greenhouse to keep the plants from freezing.

- Really good greenhouses can be purchsed from a manufacturer and can be expensive.

ECONOMICS

Materials Costs: The materials to build this greenhouse should cost in the range of $6.00–$20.00 per square foot, depending on the quality and durability of materials used.

Fuel Reduction: Each square foot of glass of your greenhouse can save from ¼ to ½ gallon of fuel oil heating season.

Cost-effectiveness: On the 1–20 scale, this suggestion earns a rating of 6–10.

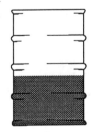

Glassed in Porches

A well shaded open porch can be a cool and comfortable place to relax in the summer. But you may want to consider changing that open porch into a closed porch. If you need more winter-time living space, a sunny glassed in porch is an inexpensive solution — and it will give you heat too. Like a sunspace, a glassed in porch traps heat while the sun shines. You can let the solar heated air from the porch into your house through a window or a new duct opening high on the wall, which can be closed at night.

The extra heat from the porch will be noticed most in the room next to it, during the daytime. The unglazed surfaces — ceilings and walls — should be heavily insulated. An insulated porch with two layers of glass will reduce the heat loss through the house wall. Every time you open a door in the winter you lose heat and money. If the porch is attached to your house entrance, it becomes an airlock entry, a buffer zone between the indoors and outdoors. The solar heated air, not the expensively heated indoor air, escapes from the open porch door.

You don't want the porch to make your house hotter in the summer. To avoid the low angle of the sun's intense heat in the morning and afternoon, you will want very little glass on the east and west sides of the porch — or even no glazing there. South-facing windows should be completely shaded during the cooling season. You should build vents to the outside on the east and west walls, equivalent in size to 20 percent of the floor area. Alternatively, design the glazing in a way that you can convert back to a screened-in porch in summer.

A porch on the north side of your home will not act as a solar collector, but it can help cut heat losses by acting as a buffer between the house and the cold outside.

VARIATIONS
- If you cannot afford to cover the porch with glass, use plastic. However, try to avoid plastics because they are not durable and can be easily damaged by wind.

ADVANTAGES
- You achieve energy savings with very little money. But remember, this glassed-in porch gets very cool on cold nights if there is no other heating system.
- It adds a cheerful, sunny extra room that can be used for many months of the year.

DISADVANTAGES
- You have to shade and vent the porch carefully so that it doesn't overheat in the summer and make the house hotter.

- The porch primarily heats only adjacent rooms. If a distant room needs heat, additional ducting and possibly a fan become necessary. This means more cost and complications.
- The porch may block sunshine from rooms that were previously well-lit.

ECONOMICS

Materials Costs: Assuming that your porch does not need a great deal of structural alteration, it could cost you about $1,000 to close it in with south-facing glass and to add the appropriate insulation. The cost will range from $6.00 to $10.00 per square foot of floor area.

Fuel Reduction: You can save as much from reduced air infiltration and the porch's insulating role as you do from solar gain through the windows. As a rough guide, though, you can figure fuel savings of ¼–½ gallon of oil per square foot of south glass for a heating season.

Cost-Effectivceness: On a scale of 1–20, this idea rates a 6–10.

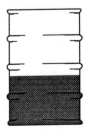

Wall Heaters

To build this air heating solar energy collector you need to have a wood frame house with a wall that faces within 30 degrees of south. Make sure that the wall is not shaded during the heating season.

On a section of the wall, between the windows and the doors, you can build a panel roughly 3' x 6' that will heat the room behind it. The design is an airtight wooden frame that holds a black metal heat absorber plate with two layers of glass in front of it. Behind the plate, cut upper and lower vents in the wall.

During the day sunlight shines through the glass and strikes the black heat absorber plate. As this heats up, it warms the air already in the panel. The warmed air starts to rise. This draws air from your house in through the lower inlet vent and past the plate. As this air heats up, it rises and flows out of the top outlet vent and into the house, where it warms the room.

This wall heater system works without a fan to move the air. Whenever the sun is shining, air will circulate by a natural flow process called thermosiphoning: warm air rises and cool air falls. A simple, lightweight backdraft damper installed over the bottom vent prevents the warm air inside your house from flowing out into the panel at night.

With the top vent open during the day, this solar design will heat your house during the cold months of fall, winter and spring. In the cooling season, close the upper vent to keep unwanted heat from circulating into the room, and shade the front of the panel.

Although the design is simple, allow yourself plenty of time to build the system. Don't cut framing members in your wall, and look out for electric wires.

VARIATIONS
- You can build up to three of these 3' x 6' sections. If you want a larger wall heater panel, with more than 60 square feet of glass, consider a fan-assisted wall heater. (See the next section.)

ADVANTAGES
- The panel is relatively inexpensive and can be built with readily available materials.
- It will operate maintenance-free for years. Just keep the glass clean.
- It doesn't lose heat at night.

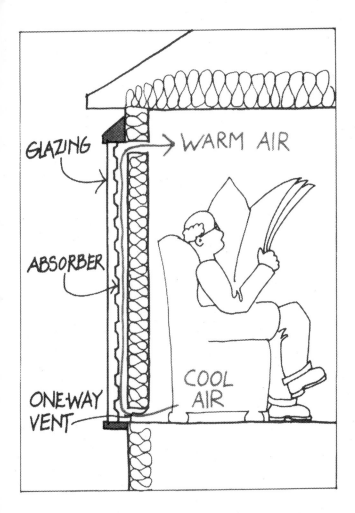

GLAZING

WARM AIR

ABSORBER

COOL AIR

ONE-WAY VENT

DISADVANTAGES
- It provides heat only during the daytime.
- You need experience with carpentry and glass installation.

ECONOMICS
Materials Costs: You can build a 45–50 square foot unit for $400–$600.

Fuel Reduction: Forty-five square feet of wall heater will save $25.00 to $50.00 per year.

Cost-Effectiveness: On a scale of 1–20, this idea rates an 8–9.

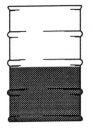

Wall Heaters with a Fan

For this wall heater, you will need a lot of uninterrupted wall area that faces south — enough to hold four or more sections of wall heater (see previous page) roughly 3' x 6' each. Each section is an airtight frame that holds a black metal absorber plate with two layers of glass in front of it.

Operating the heater is very simple. During the day, sunlight shines through the glass, strikes the heat absorber plate, and heats it up. When the absorber plate reaches about 90 degrees Fahrenheit, a thermostat connected to the plate turns on a fan. The fan draws air from the house through a lower vent at one end of the heater. The air travels up the absorber plate, out the upper vent at the end opposite the inlet vent, and into your house.

When the sun is not shining, the thermostat turns off the wall heater fan automatically and dampers stop the airflow between the house and the heater. During late spring, summer, and early fall, turn the thermostat way down and disconnect the power to the fan. Then completely shade the wall heater, if possible, with an awning, a bamboo screen or whitewash on the glass.

Building this wall heater requires skills in residential carpentry, glazing installation, ducting, and wiring. Before you start buying materials, have your local building inspector check your plans. Be careful when you cut into your walls.

VARIATIONS
• You can build any size system your south wall can accomodate.

ADVANTAGES
• The system will last for years and requires little maintenance: cleaning the glass, painting the frame, and lubricating and maintaining the fan.
• This solar design puts out a lot of heat.

DISADVANTAGES
• It provides heat only during the daytime.
• It takes construction experience to build.
• The system does use some electricity to operate, though very little.
• It may eliminate direct sunlight entering the house.

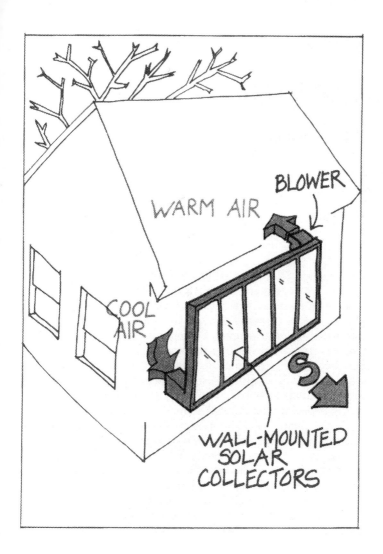

ECONOMICS

Materials Costs: Wall heaters cost between $10.00 and $13.00 per square foot to make, and an average unit (110 square feet) costs about $1,000 to $1,400.

Fuel Reduction: A 100 square foot collector will save 40 to 100 gallons of oil per year.

Cost Effectiveness: On a scale of 1–20, this idea rates an 8–9.

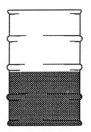

Lean-to Collectors With Storage

This project uses a south-facing lean-to as a solar heat collector. It differs from some of the other projects because it can store heat for later use.

The surface of the lean-to is painted flat-black to collect heat and is covered with glass or plastic. Rocks of approximately uniform size are placed inside to absorb and save heat for later use. Use about one cubic foot of rock per square foot of collector area. The rock should be approximately uniform in size and be about one inch in diameter.

This is an air heating collector — it uses air as the collecting and circulating medium. Air is warmed when it touches the hot black surface. A blower draws hot air from the collector down through the rock pile. Cooled air returns from the rocks, through concrete blocks turned on their ends, to the collector. When warm air is needed in the house, another fan draws air up through the warm rocks and into the house. It is important to use the proper fan size. If your fan is too large, you will use excessive electricity, reducing your overall energy savings.

Make sure all ducts are air-tight. The rock-bin should also be air-tight, and its bottom, top and sides well insulated. The back of the solar absorbing surface should be well insulated so that heat stored in the rocks does not escape. Include a vent when you design the lean-to. A vent allows excess heat to escape in the summer.

VARIATIONS
- This structure need not be mounted flat against a wall. It can be free standing and ducted to the room needing heat. If you build a steeply pitched lean-to, place reflecting surfaces in front to increase the solar gain.

WHERE THIS WORKS
The most suitable place for a combined lean-to solar collector and rock storage system is on a south wall that has few windows. If your house collects enough heat through its windows during a winter day, this lean-to can store extra heat for nighttime use.

ADVANTAGES
- This structure needs no major changes to the interior of the house. You only add two air ducts through the wall and a fan control switch.
- Because this structure is insulated and warm, it further insulates the existing wall against which it is placed.
- The storage bin allows you to save daytime heat for use when it is needed most at night.

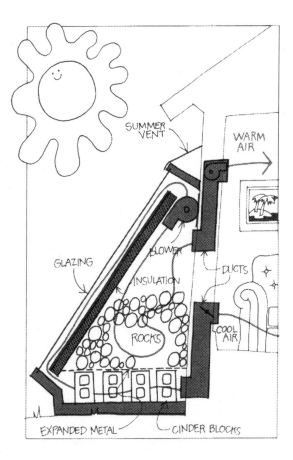

Labels in figure: SUMMER VENT, WARM AIR, GLAZING, BLOWER, INSULATION, DUCTS, ROCKS, COOL AIR, EXPANDED METAL, CINDER BLOCKS

DISADVANTAGES

- In some cases you must build a foundation under the lean-to, which adds to the cost.
- This device is more complex than some of the other projects. This increases cost and maintenance while lowering cost-effectiveness.

ECONOMICS

Materials Costs: The materials to build your lean-to include plywood, paint, glass or other glazing, insulation, concrete blocks, rocks, ductwork, fan and miscellaneous vents, controls and finishes. The cost should run from $10.00 to $20.00 per square foot of collecting surface. This applies for a unit of medium size (100–200 square feet).

Fuel Reduction: With a medium sized unit, 100 square feet of collector can save about 50–100 gallons of oil per heating season, or ½ to 1 gallon per square foot.

Cost-effectiveness: On the 1–20 scale, this suggestion earns a rating of 7–9.

Introduction

As much as 20 percent of the energy used in our homes heats our water for washing and bathing. The sun can help supply that energy. However, the first step is to cut back on what we use.

In a typical U.S. household, each person uses about 20 gallons of hot water per day. This is significantly higher than the rest of the world uses. You can cut down tremendously without sacrificing at all, saving energy — and money.

You can reduce water use in a number of ways. About 50 percent of the hot water we use is for bathing, about 25 percent is for laundry, and the rest is for cooking, lavatory, and miscellaneous cleaning. A shower uses far less water than a bath. You save even more with a water-conserving shower head that gives off a spray of water rather than a hard steady stream. If you cut hot water for bathing by 50 percent, you cut your water heating bill by 25 percent.

You can save on laundry hot water by only washing full loads and by using cooler water temperatures for washing and cold for rinsing, even for white loads.

In the kitchen, rinse dishes in a basin of hot water rather than under a steady stream of tap water. Or use a faucet aerator with a simple switch for flipping the water on and off quickly and easily.

Once you cut your hot water use as much as possible, then look to the sun for heating the water you really do need. This is usually best done by using solar energy to preheat the water. This means that it gets first crack at heating the water, before the conventional water heater does it. To whatever extent the sun first heats your water — partially or completely — you save energy. If the sun heats the water somewhat but not totally, the conventional heater takes over and heats it to the required temperature.

Solar water heating is very easy. A garden hose sitting in the sun is perhaps the simplest example of a solar water heater, but it does not heat water very efficiently or make it very hot. Nor does it store it for later when the sun isn't shining. Solving these drawbacks complicates solar heating systems. An unfailing supply of hot water requires a conventional backup energy source. Nevertheless, solar water heaters are practical and a good solar project.

In addition, solar hot water heaters have another important economic advantage. While solar house heaters sit idle during the warm months, solar water heaters are needed year-round. They save you money every time the sun is shining. And, as we've seen, water heating is a large part of your total energy bill.

Solar hot water heating collectors are similar to other collectors in most respects. The major construction difference, besides their smaller size, is that hot water heaters, because they operate all year-round, should be tilted to make good use of both winter and summer sun. Tilt them at an angle equal to your latitude. For example, if you live at a latitude of 35 degrees, tilt your collectors about 35 degrees from horizontal.

The easiest collector for you to build would probably be ½ inch copper tubes soldered 6 inches apart to a thin copper sheet painted black and mounted in an insulated box with two layers of glass on top.

The biggest technical problem, common to nearly all solar hot water heaters, is the danger of freezing. Of the four types of heaters, from simple to complex, the Batch Heater is the simplest and avoids the freezing problem entirely. It is drained and left empty during the months when freezing is likely. The Drainback System solves the problem by letting the water drain out of the collectors when the pump stops. The Pumped System uses a non-freezing solution in the collectors. The Thermosiphon is similar to the pumped system, except it is designed to avoid the need for a pump.

Solar water heating seems simple, but there are many technical challenges such as freezing and corrosion. Numerous minor problems can arise. You will need to be experienced in carpentry, metal work, plumbing, and electrical work. However, many people can build a solar hot water heater; it can be simple and cheap, and it's worth doing. You'll save money and learn a lot. Before you start to build your water heater, read the references listed in the *Appendix*. And, of course, there's always the other option of buying a commercially made and installed system. See Pages 60 to 64 for advice on what to look for.

Batch Heaters

A batch heater (sometimes called a breadbox) is a water tank painted black, mounted in a well insulated box, and covered by a sheet of glazing. The batch heater preheats the cold water from your well or municipal water supply, reducing the amount of energy your water heater uses. The best location for a batch heater is an unshaded area in the yard on the south side of your home or as close as possible to your existing tank.

The sun's energy passes through the glazing and is absorbed by the black surface of the tank. This heat is immediately transferred to the colder water in the tank, supplied from your well or municipal water service. On a warm sunny summer day, the water in the tank may reach 140 degrees Fahrenheit. This preheated water then flows to a well insulated outlet pipe to your home's water heater. As the warm water is delivered to your home, it is replaced in the tank by cold water from the inlet pipe and the cycle continues.

To get the most hot water from this solar system, use only a single layer of glass. Including a reflector in the design will increase the amount of solar energy the tank receives. The water lines going to and from the solar tank should be well insulated and kept as short as possible .

The batch heater is drained at the first sign of a severe frost and refilled in the spring when all danger of frost has passed. This heater requires just about zero maintenance — every two years add a fresh coat of paint and check the sacrificial rod that is placed in the tank to reduce corrosion.

A batch heater is an excellent choice for a water heating system. It's inexpensive and takes a moderate amount of experience with carpentry and plumbing to build. It will pay for itself very quickly, especially if it is combined with the hot water conservation measures. The batch heater is flexible — if you have a sunny wall, you can build a freestanding version.

Some commercial solar water heaters you can purchase are based on this design. By using advanced materials, they do not freeze in the winter and can be used year round.

VARIATIONS
- The batch heater can be oriented in a north-south direction or it can also stretch in an east-west direction.
- Purchased versions of this design use several layers of glazing and operate year round

ADVANTAGES
- This hot water system is the cheapest and simplest to build. For the cost it puts out a good amount of hot water.

DISADVANTAGES
- The total hot water production is lower than some other systems because the batch heater is not used all year.

ECONOMICS
Materials costs: Construction of a batch heater, including $50.00 for energy conservation measures on your existing hot water system, will cost between $500 and $1000.

Fuel Reduction: A batch heater can cut your hot water bill by half when it operates, or up to 1200 kWh per year.

Cost-Effectiveness: On the scale of 1–20, this suggestions earns a rating of 10–12.

Drainback Systems

A drainback system can provide up to 70 percent of the hot water for a family of four. The system has two solar collectors, a small storage tank, and control mechanisms. When the sun shines, its energy passes through the glass on the collectors and strikes the black heat absorber plate. A pump circulates the water to be heated from the storage tank to the collector. Several gallons of water continuously circulate in a loop from the collectors to the storage tank. The cold water supply enters into the coiled tubes of a heat exchanger submersed in the storage tank. As it passes through the exchanger on its way to your water heater, the water picks up heat from the water in the storage tank.

The south-facing collectors can be mounted on your roof or on a rack in your yard. To reduce costly pipe runs, they should be as close as possible to your present water heater. Whenever the collectors are no longer warmed by the sun, the pump stops. The water in the loop then automatically "drains back" by gravity from the collectors and piping into the storage tank. The collectors need to be higher than the storage tank to ensure that the system will drain properly.

Maintenance for the drainback system is simple: washing the collector glass occasionally, lubricating the pump, and checking the various parts of the system to make sure they are well-insulated and operating properly.

ADVANTAGES
- It has a simple freeze protection system that doesn't require costly non-freezing liquids.
- Although this system is more costly than the batch heater, its output is greater.

DISADVANTAGES
- This system requires careful design and thorough engineering, but there may be a local expert who could help.

ECONOMICS
Materials Costs: A drainback system of about 32 square feet will cost between $700 and $1,000, including a $50.00 investment in conservation measures for your existing system.

Fuel Reduction: With 32 square feet of collector area, you can expect to cut your annual hot water bill by $100 or more.

Cost-Effectiveness: On a scale of 1–20, this suggestions rates an 8–11.

SOLAR COLLECTORS

PUMP

HOT WATER

COLD WATER

Pumped Systems

These systems are very similar to drain back systems except that a non-freezing liquid rather than water is pumped through the collectors. When the collectors get cold, the liquid remains rather than draining out. A small pump circulates the liquid through the collector when the sun is out. This allows you to place the storage tank anywhere in the house. You can use ½ inch piping throughout. The pump moves less than 50 gallons per hour, so operating costs are low.

The collector is similar to that used in the thermosiphoning design. Allow 10–15 square feet of collector per person.

AUXILIARY HEATING ARRANGEMENT

This arrangement works for either a pumped-water or thermosiphoning system. If you want a constant supply of hot water, treat the collector as a pre-heater for your conventional water heater. The conventional heater will act as an auxiliary and turn on only when needed, usually on cloudy days.

Two tanks are used in the best arrangement, with the solar storage tank serving as a preheat supply tank for the conventional hot water heater. The size of the tank depends on the size of your family. Allow 10–20 gallons per person.

ECONOMICS

Materials cost: This system is slightly more expensive than the thermosiphoning one. The cost difference is for the pump, a control devise, and some additional plumbing. Figure $20.00–$35.00 per square foot of collector.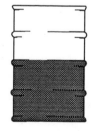
Fuel Reduction: A good unit can save from 1½–2½ gallons of oil per square foot per year or 60–100 kWh per square foot per year.
Cost-effectiveness: On our scale of 1–20, this suggestion earns a rating of 8–11.

Thermosiphoning Collectors

This is simlar to the drainback and pumped systems except that it doesn't need a pump. The water circulates by thermosiphoning, or natural circulation. Warm liquid from the collector rises and cooler liquid from the tank settles down in a slow, continuous flow from collector to tank to collector.

To facilitate this flow, use large piping (½–1 inch diameter) between collector and tank; keep the number of bends and elbows to a minimum, and mount the tank 2 feet higher than the top of the collector to prevent reverse flow at night.

To prevent freezing, use a non-freezing fluid which moves through a heat exchanger that transfers heat to the water in the tank. Insulate the tank well (8–10 inches) to minimize heat loss. Because the tank must be above the collector, it often ends up on the roof or in your attic. If this happens, make sure your building can support its weight. You can change the appearance of the tank enclosure by disguising it, for example, as a chimney.

AUXILIARY HEATING ARRANGEMENT
See *Pumped Water Systems*.

ECONOMICS
Materials Costs: This system is similar in cost to the drainback and pumped systems, around $1,000 for making it yourself, including a $50.00 investment in conservation measures for your existing system.
Fuel Reduction: With 32 square feet of collector area, you can expect to cut your annual hot water bill in half, saving as much as $100 or more.
Cost-Effectiveness: On a scale of 1–20, this suggestions rates an 8–11.

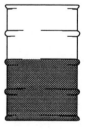

HEAT
EXCHANGER

WARM
WATER

NON-
FREEZING
SYSTEM

COPPER
ABSORBER
& TUBING,
PAINTED
BLACK

COOL
WATER

WATER
SYSTEM

Roof Trickle Collectors

If you have a south-sloping roof that needs repair, you might consider converting it to a trickle-type solar collector that uses water to gather solar heat for your home. Cover your roof with a black-painted sheet metal, such as corrugated aluminum. Cover the assembly with glass or plastic. Pump water from a storage tank and let it trickle slowly over it to absorb its heat. Collect the heated water at the bottom and drain it back into the tank. Leave the tank uninsulated but place it in an insulated closet-like space. Blow house air through the closet and voila — solar home heat!

A pump forces the water from the storage tank to the collector. A ½–¾ inch diameter pipe perforated with tiny holes is placed along the crest of the roof and squirts water down each of the troughs in the corrugated metal.

The metal sheet can get very hot when water is not flowing over it. Make sure the sheet does not touch a part of your old roof that is unable to withstand high temperatures (like tar paper or asphalt shingles). In fact, placing insulation between the roof and the metal sheet will increase the efficiency of your collector and protect your roof.

One layer of glass is sufficient. Make your collector air and water-tight and insure that it is self-draining when the sun is not shining. Otherwise, water will freeze and the pipes will burst.

VARIATIONS
- There are several other ways to move the heat from the storage tank to the house. The warm water can circulate through pipes buried in floors or ceilings. You can submerge the tank in a rock bin and then blow air through the bin and into the house. The method you choose depends on your particular situation.

WHERE THIS WORKS
This project is applicable to sunny south-facing roofs.

ADVANTAGES
- Because of the large area of roof used for collection, this system can supply a large amount of your heat. It will reduce heat loss through your roof, providing additional savings.
- It can be used all year round to preheat your domestic hot water.
- This is one of the simplest types of water heating solar collectors you can make.

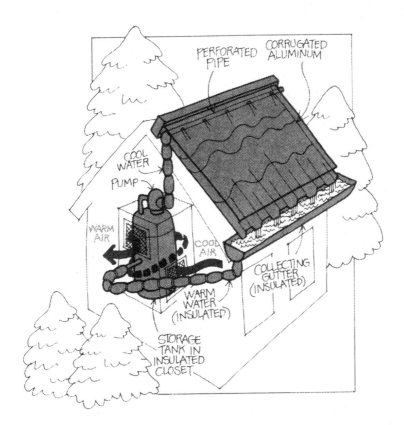

Labels in figure:
PERFORATED PIPE
CORRUGATED ALUMINUM
COOL WATER
PUMP
WARM AIR
COOL AIR
COLLECTING GUTTER (INSULATED)
WARM WATER (INSULATED)
STORAGE TANK IN INSULATED CLOSET

DISADVANTAGES

- The storage tank requires space in the cellar or house, sometimes as much as a small room.
- The system is quite complex, requiring piping, a pump, a fan, and automatic controls to regulate the collector.

ECONOMICS

Materials Costs: The materials to build this collector and heat-storage unit, including sheet metal, glazing, piping, structure and water pump, will cost about $10.00–$25.00 per square foot of collector area. This applies to systems in the 200–400 square foot range.

Fuel Reduction: Each square foot of this solar collector can be expected to save from ⅓–⅔ gallon of fuel oil each winter. For 200 square feet of collector and oil costing $1.50 per gallon, yearly savings range from $100–200.

Cost-effectiveness: On the 1–20 scale, this suggestion earns a rating of 6–8.

Note: This concept is patented. Construction plans are available from Edmund Scientific Co., Barrington, New Jersey

Solar Heating Systems Using Conventional Hot Water Heaters

If you are considering a small (200 square feet or less) addition to your house, this is an idea for heating that addition — using the sun. The system uses an oversized conventional water heater to store heated water collected with solar collectors. The standard heating element provides back-up heat. The sun actually preheats the water and halves the amount of heat the conventional system must produce.

Before trying this scheme, design the addition with maximum south-facing windows; face the roof toward the winter sun to provide a location for the solar collectors; insulate the building thoroughly.

This solar system requires a water-heating collector mounted to face the winter sun. A pump circulates water through the collectors to a conventional, well-insulated hot water tank with an attached water-to-air heat exchanger coil. When the room needs heat, a fan circulates room air over these warmed coils and back into the room. As a rule-of-thumb, use up to 60 square feet of solar collector for a well-insulated 200 square foot addition. Provide up to 2 gallons of water storage for each square foot of solar collector.

VARIATIONS
- Instead of using an insulated tank, you can place an uninsulated tank in an insulated closet. When heat is required in the living spaces, open the closet doors and let the hot tank radiate heat into the room.
- The solar heated water can be circulated through finned baseboard heaters in each room.

WHERE THIS WORKS
This works best in a well-insulated building. Place the heat storage closet centrally to allow easy circulation of warm air. The system is appropriate only for small buildings because the storage capacity of an 80 gallon domestic hot-water tank is small. You need larger components for a space larger than 250 square feet.

ADVANTAGES
- This system uses readily available, familiar equipment.
- When you use pumps and blowers to move heat around, you have greater freedom in locating systems components.

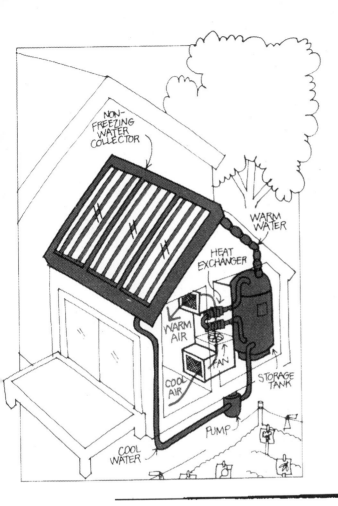

DISADVANTAGES

- This is a relatively expensive way to use solar energy.
- The storage tank and ductwork take up space. In a small building, this could be a problem.

ECONOMICS

Materials Costs: A system like this requires many plumbing supplies, driving costs up to the range of from $20.00 to $40.00 per square foot of collector.

Fuel Reduction: Because this system has storage, you can regulate and use the heat when you need it most. Savings are ½–1 gallon of oil per square foot per season or 50–100 gallons for a 100 square foot system.

Cost-effectiveness: On the 1–20 scale, this suggestion earns a rating of 6–7.

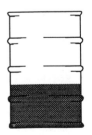

Warm Air Collectors Without Storage

This idea is for an air solar collector which cannot store heat for later use. Air collectors work well in a free-standing structure where a liquid system might freeze.

Here, cool room air is delivered through insulated ducts to the collector bottom. As it rises over the collecting surface the air warms and then returns to your house through another insulated duct at the top of the collector.

You usually need a fan to blow the air through the collector and back to the house. Sometimes, however, the air will rise naturally by thermosiphoning. The fan should blow 2–3 cubic feet of air per minute, per square foot of glass in the collector. Constructing your own air solar collector is tricky, but you can learn how.

VARIATIONS
- Enhance your collector's appearance by combining the warm and cool air ducts in one structure and running them underground.
- Your collector will look and work better if you attach it directly onto another structure such as a porch or a storage shed. This also cuts the collector cost.
- Place a large reflector on the ground in front of the collector to increase the heat output.

WHERE THIS WORKS
In densely populated areas or in residences that share walls with other buildings, a free-standing collector is often the only solar device that can be used. If you can place the solar collector about two feet lower than the rooms you plan to heat, you can take advantage of thermosiphoning — heat's natural flow — and reduce the need for a fan.

ADVANTAGES
- Because this collector is free-standing, you can orient it due south and tilt it at its optimal angle.
- A separate collector does not alter the structure or appearance of the building its heating.
- You can easily shut the collector off during the summertime.

DISADVANTAGES
- Ducts can lose heat. You should insulate them with the equivalent of at least 6 inches of fiberglass insulation.

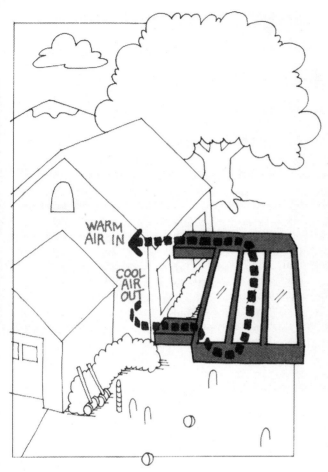

- For the energy provided, a free-standing collector is often more expensive than an integral or attached one. The support structure and the ductwork from the collector to the house will add cost.

ECONOMICS

Materials Costs: The materials, such as glass or plastic, wood, paint, absorbing surface and ductwork, for a solar collector and structure of 100 square feet cost from $1,000 to $2,000 or $10.00 to $20.00 per square foot. This figure can vary substantially with the quality of the collector you build.

Fuel Reduction: With this medium-sized unit, you can expect annual savings of ⅓–¾ gallon of fuel oil for each square foot of collector, or 33–75 gallons for the entire unit.

Cost-effectiveness: On the 1–20 scale, this suggestion earns a rating of 7–10.

Solar Water Heaters And Garden Sheds With Heat Storage

Build a storage shed in your backyard. Place a collector on the south-facing surface. Attach an insulated hot water tank horizontally about 18 inches above the top of the collector. A reflector above the collector surface increases the solar radiation on the collectors. Since the water storage is higher than the top of the collectors, the system can use thermosiphoning for water circulation. Hot water is pumped to the house and used as needed. The back side of the structure is a garden shed with doors.

You will have to look elsewhere for the specific details of your water collector, but basically you will want to build a glazed box that contains a blackened, heat-conducting metal surface with pipes attached to it (for best results use copper). Solar heat is absorbed by the black metal and transferred to the water in the pipes which then carries it to the storage tank or house.

You can make the collector in 8-foot-long sections out of standard dimension building material. For this length collector, your water storage tank should be roughly 24 inches in diameter. Insulate the back of your collector to reduce heat loss and boost collector efficiency. Also, be sure to make provisions to avoid the freezing of pipes in the wintertime.

VARIATIONS
- You can easily change the size of the shed, both in height and length, as long as the proportions are kept about the same.
- To increase the collector's output, add a reflector on the ground in front of it.

WHERE THIS WORKS
Any free-standing device works best where the building to be heated receives too little sunlight. The existing heating system must also be considered. You can combine the device with a water-to-air heat exchanger coil to produce hot air for house heating. With greater difficulty and expense, you can combine the project with an existing hot water baseboard heating system. Most conventional heating systems use higher temperature water than this solar collector provides. Therefore, the baseboard system must be enlarged to compensate for the lower temperatures from the collector. Other options such as radiant panel heating also may be possible.

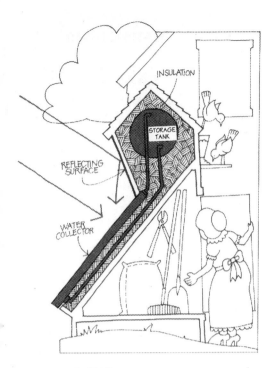

ADVANTAGES
- By combining the collector with a shed, some of the costs of the solar system (structural framing and foundation costs) can be shared with shed costs.

DISADVANTAGES
- This system needs protection against freezing. You can circulate an non-freezing solution through the collector and then through a heat exchanger in the storage tank or you can drain the system on freezing nights.
- A free standing collector loses more heat than one attached to the building.
- This system demands more skill in design and building than many of the simpler ones. See *Appendix* for help.

ECONOMICS
Materials Costs: The materials for 100 square feet of collector will cost $2,000–$3,000 or $20.00–$30.00 per square foot. This includes costs for the shed and the insulated pipe to the house, but no extra amount for new heating systems, if required

Fuel Reduction: During each heating season, savings can be from ½–1 gallon of fuel oil per square foot of collector or 50–100 gallons for a 100 square foot model.

Cost-effectiveness: On the 1–20 scale. this suggestion earns a rating of 7–8.

Garages

A new building simplifies your task of "going solar." It is far easier to design and construct a new building with solar than to convert, or retrofit, an existing one. Even if the new building, like a garage, does not need heat, it can provide space for the collectors and heat storage. To simplify heat circulation, the new structure should be relatively close to the rooms using the solar heat.

The storage area, even when heavily insulated, loses some heat. So whenever possible, it is more efficient to place the storage in the house. Then the lost heat is not wasted — it is "lost" to the living spaces which need it anyway.

If you use an air solar collector, you will store heat in a rock bin. The rocks should be uniform in size with diameters of 1½ to 2½ inches. Solar heated air from the collector should feed directly to an air space at the top of the rock bin. To retrieve the heat, draw it from the top of your storage bin. The air should move in a direction opposite to the one in which it was delivered This is a project for which most people will need more information than can be given here.

VARIATIONS
• There are endless ways to use new structures as partial solar collectors. A new barn, trash shed, billboard or picnic shed can support a solar collector. At the same time there are almost as many places where your heat storage can go. One well-known solar pioneer placed 16-foot-high rock storage tubes in the entrance foyer of his house. Use your imagination!

WHERE THIS WORKS
A variety of places are suitable. The main point is that solar collection can be integrated with a new building and greatly reduce the cost of the solar system. Any of the other schemes in this book can be applied to a new building; this one is unique because a new structure supplies heat for the existing building. This idea is particularly suitable if, by adding a new structure, you can achieve a better solar orientation.

ADVANTAGES
• An existing building is often not ideally suited for solar collectors. But when you build from scratch, it is much easier to integrate solar heating with the design.
• A good collector and storage system is the most efficient way to store solar heat for more than one day.

DISADVANTAGES

- This project requires engineering skills that are often beyond the grasp of many homeowners. Do not be too discouraged; the more you work with it, the better you will get!
- This project also carries a high price tag. If you cannot afford the entire bill now, design with solar in mind and install the system later.
- The high cost of this system makes it less cost-effective than simpler ones.

ECONOMICS

Materials Costs: It is almost impossible to estimate the cost of an undefined system. However, it would certainly be one of the most expensive. A good guess for materials is between $15.00 and $25.00 per square foot.

Fuel Reduction: A well-made collector and storage system can save ½–1 gallon of fuel oil per square foot each heating season.

Cost-effectiveness: On the 1–20 scale, this suggestion earns a rating of 6–9.

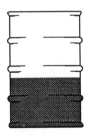

Thermal Mass

So far, this book has offered ways to make houses better collectors and conservers of solar energy. If your house overheats from too much sunshine, consider making your house store the excess heat for later use. You can do this by placing a substantial amount of heat-holding material such as masonry, concrete or containers of water where the sun can shine on them. This thermal mass will help to prevent the sunny room from being overheated and will reduce the need for opening windows or shading out the sun's free energy just to maintain comfort. At night, this mass will re-radiate its stored solar heat and reduce the need for conventional heat.

There are many ways to add thermal mass to a room. The challenge is to add enough. Try to provide 2 to 4 gallons (¼ to ½ cubic feet) of water per square foot of south window, or ½ to 1 cubic foot (75 to 150 lbs.) of concrete or masonry per square foot. If the mass is not in direct sunlight, double or triple these amounts. If you have a concrete slab, you already have plenty of thermal mass — just allow the sun to reach it. The mass should be dark-colored to absorb radiation and should be placed as close to the window as possible so that the sunshine hits it all day.

VARIATIONS
- If you have a strong floor, you can pour a thin 2"–4" concrete slab over it, or lay down brick or heavy tile.
- Steel drums or racks of water-filled containers could act as partitions or furniture.
- An interior wall that receives sunlight could be lined with stone or brick.
- Thermal mass in shady areas will also help by moderating temperatures. When you lower your thermostat at night, the mass stays warmer for several hours keeping the space warm too.

WHERE THIS WORKS
Adding thermal mass is best for rooms with lots of southern sun (especially those that overheat). The thermal mass must be placed in unobstructed sunlight for as many hours a day as possible.

ADVANTAGES
- The addition of thermal mass does not increase the amount of solar energy available to a space, but it lengthens the time over which you can use the heat .
- Thermal mass moderates temperature swings between day and night keeping the space more comfortable.
- Excess heat that might otherwise be thrown away is saved and used later.
- Thermal mass has no moving or complex processes. It simply sits there and does its job without your time or effort.

30-GALLON
DRUM WITH
WATER

DISADVANTAGES

- Thermal mass requires bulky materials and often takes up a lot of space. It's often exceedingly difficult to add more in a graceful way that's acceptable to your existing decor.
- The structure of your house will most likely need strengthening before it can support the considerable weight of thermal mass. To be sure, have your house checked before you load in the mass.

ECONOMICS

Materials Costs: Thermal mass materials are common and inexpensive. Concrete runs $40.00 to $60.00 per cubic yard (27 cubic feet). Water is almost free. Containers, such as steel drums or plastic jugs, can be scrounged or bought secondhand. Figure $1.00 to $2.00 per square foot of window area.

Fuel Reduction: Thermal mass reduces fuel consumption only in that it makes the solar energy available through your windows more usable. If the windows don't overheat the space, the mass won't help, except by moderating uncomfortable temperature change. On the other hand, under good conditions, thermal mass will save from $1/10$ to $1/5$ gallons of oil per square foot of south window per heating season.

Cost-effectiveness: On the 1–20 scale, this suggestion earns a rating of 6–9.

Buying a Commercial System

How do you decide which solar energy system to build or buy for your house? The choices range from do-it-yourself projects to commercially available equipment and complex systems. They all guarantee energy savings, and some companies may even promise energy independence.

Price tags and predicted payback periods are only two of the many pieces of information that a homeowner must consider before making a decision. Suppose that you don't have the time, or perhaps the skills, to install one of the do-it-yourself systems described in this booklet... but you definitely want to take advantage of the sun to cut your energy costs. How do you begin to go shopping for a commercial solar system?

GETTING READY

The very first step is to do an energy audit on your home. There are several places where you can find an auditor qualified to do this energy analysis for you. Try your local utility, other local fuel suppliers, private consultants trained in energy auditing, or solar contractors. Ask your state energy office for lists of auditors in your state.

An energy audit is usually low cost and sometimes even free. The trained energy advisor will survey your home from top to bottom and locate the areas where energy is being wasted. Then the advisor will write out recommendations for making your home more energy efficient, usually with an estimate for the cost of different measures. Making your home energy efficient is the essential first step before adding any solar systems.

Step two is to evaluate your site. If your house faces south, or within 30 degrees of south, you may be able to get enough energy from the sun to make the investment worthwhile. Shading is very important to consider. You don't ever want your solar water collector to be shaded by trees or by nearby buildings. But passive solar space heating systems need to be unshaded in the winter and shaded in the summer.

Luckily, the siting of hot water collectors is flexible. Even if your roof doesn't face south, the collectors can be mounted on racks on your roof and angled to face south. Or they can be mounted on racks in your yard facing south. If the system you want must go on your house, you need adequate space on your roof or south-facing walls.

Will it be convenient to route insulated pipes or ductwork through your house? You may need an extra hot water storage tank and possibly a heat exchanger — is there room near your present hot water heater? You'll get the most out of a passive space heating system if you can put materials that store heat in your house: perhaps a brick wall, a concrete slab floor, tubes or large drums filled with water, or even a rockbed in the basement. Would you have any space to add some heat storage material for your space heating system?

GOING SHOPPING

Comparison shopping is the name of the game. Keep in mind that you are the customer, and the installer should be more than willing to devote time to answering every one of your questions. By the time you sign your name on the dotted line, there should be no doubt in your mind that this is the best system possible for the price you want to pay.

Consult with several solar contractors. The installer's location is important. Is there a local office that can respond promptly to service calls? Check out the firm's local reputation. Ask for references and check them. Are these customers satisfied with their installation and the way their system has worked? If there were some problems, how serious were they and how quickly was the service call answered?

If possible, visit some installations. Look for overall neatness, simple plumbing arrangements, and small touches like tagged and labeled pipes and drains. Ask for a diagram that shows how the system works. What kind of controls are used — what regulates the temperature and how does the system turn on and off? What kind of freeze protection is there?

Make sure you understand how the system works. Where does the installer recommend that the collectors be placed? How will they look? What are the advantages and disadvantages of a particular mounting method? Will it meet state and local building codes? Will the piping to and from the collectors be visible? Will the pipes and tank be insulated? Can your present hot water tank be used?

Find out what the total installed cost, including sales tax, will be. Ask for an estimate of the annual energy savings. Taking tax credits — if any — into consideration, in how many years will the system pay for itself?

Find out what you have to do to maintain the system. Does the installer provide service, repair and parts for the system? What will service calls cost after the warranty has expired? Is a maintenance contract available? Ask for a copy of the warranty and read it carefully. What is covered and for what periods of time? You should expect at least a one-year warranty on parts and labor. Warranties should be transferrable to a new owner of the house. Be sure to get a homeowner's manual, with instructions for operation and maintenance, and have the installer sit down and go through it with you.

When you decide to buy a system, obtain a written agreement that the final payment will not be made until after the system has operated normally for seven days and has then been inspected by the installer.

SPACE HEATERS

"The simpler the better" is an idea that holds true when it comes to adding on solar energy equipment or systems to help heat your home. Any system that doesn't include heat storage can help heat your home only during the daytime. That means it can be expected to supply 10 to 15 percent of the total heat your house needs year round.

The types of house heating systems already mentioned in this book are the most recommended for a retrofit: a wall heater, additional windows, a sunspace, or greenhouse. Most of these systems can be provided by commercial firms too. System designs vary, so remember to do some comparison shopping.

There are two types of "active" solar space heating systems that combine collectors with heat storage: liquid and air systems. Either can be tied into a conventional forced-air heating system. The amount of heat an active system will deliver depends on the size of the collector area and the amount of storage.

Retrofitting an active space heating system can often be difficult and expensive. An average-sized system requires at least 200 square feet of collectors. For storage, a liquid system uses a large water tank, and an air system usually requires a rockbed. Either of these storage options can be difficult to add to an existing house.

The components of a liquid-based system are collectors, a pump, controls, a storage tank, and a heat exchanger. A non- freezing fluid is pumped through the collectors where it gathers heat. Then the fluid flows through a heat exchanger in the storage tank where it transfers heat to the stored water. Alternatively, water can be circulated through the system, eliminating the use of the heat exchanger in the tank. The controls will automatically drain the water back from the collectors at night or when the water in the collectors is in danger of freezing. When the collectors start gathering heat, the system will start up again.

You cannot use a solar heating system with most baseboard heating systems because baseboard radiators are designed to use higher temperatures than collectors will produce. But a liquid solar system can be easily connected to a forced hot air heating system. Water from storage will circulate through a duct mounted water-to-air heat exchanger and warm the air blown through it.

An air-based heating system consists of collectors, fans, controls, and storage, usually a rockbed. Fans blow air through the collectors and then through ducts either directly to the house if the house needs heat, or to storage if the house doesn't immediately need heat. At night the fans shut off, stopping the air flow to the collectors. When the house needs heat and the collectors are turned off, it pulls the heat from storage. If there isn't enough heat in storage, then the auxiliary heating system turns on.

Using an active solar system to heat your domestic water as well as your house means that you can use the system all year and get the most for your money. A liquid system can be connected to the domestic hot water system with a water-to-water heat exchanger. An air-based system can be connected to it with an air-to-water heat exchanger. In this case, you will need an additional pump to circulate water from the hot water tank to the heat exchanger.

Most commercial systems cost between $40.00 and $75.00 per square foot of collector (including storage costs). State tax credits — if any — may make this investment somewhat less. Assuming that you pay for electricity to heat your house at the rate of 10 cents per kWh, 100 square feet of active solar collector area added to your house could save you $160–$240 per year. When you take into account the amount of money and energy you can save by adding on an active solar system, a system costing $40.00 per square foot would pay back in 20 years.

WATER HEATERS

Using solar energy to heat your water makes better economic sense compared with solar home heating. A solar water system begins to cut your monthly fuel bills as soon as it is installed, and it operates year round. Hot water easily accounts for 20 percent of a typical family's energy consumption. Once your house is well weatherized and is using less energy for heat, hot water may account for as much as 30–40 percent of the energy you use. Conservation measures alone can often cut in half the amount of energy a family uses to heat water. (See *Solar Water Heaters*) A solar system can then supply up to two-thirds or more of the remaining energy required for hot water.

Solar collectors have been commercially available for a long time, and their price is not likely to come down. Commercially installed systems range in price, roughly from $2,000 to $4,000. A collector should last 20 years at least, if it is properly engineered and installed. For durability, the best materials are glass rather than plastic, copper rather than aluminum or steel, and an aluminum frame rather than a plastic or wooden one. Moving parts like valves will probably wear out first. Most of the other components are off-the-shelf plumbing parts. Reputable solar hot water systems all operate at relatively similar efficiencies in their ability to collect solar energy to heat water.

Factors that will affect the efficiency of the system in supplying hot water are the proper siting of the system, the use of pipe and tank insulation, and your pattern of using hot water. Doing your laundry, dishes, showers and such when the sun is shining makes the best use of the system.

SWIMMING POOL HEATERS

If you're thinking about using solar energy to heat your swimming pool, once again you should think about heat conservation first. To start, first shelter your pool from the wind, an easy and practical way to prevent heat losses. Solid fencing or shrubs can be used to protect in-ground pools from the cooling effect of the wind.

Above-ground pools also loose some heat through their side walls, and shrubs can help reduce those heat losses too. Soil banked up against the side walls of an above-ground pool will just about eliminate heat losses there, but be careful not to puncture the walls during construction.

One of the simplest and cheapest ways to raise the temperature of a swimming pool is to cover it with a sheet of clear plastic. Pool covers can help you start using your pool earlier in the spring and continue using it later in the fall. The plastic covering on the pool during the day helps it collect heat in a sunny location; in a shady place, it reduces heat losses. Transparent covers permit sunlight to enter and heat the water while any pool cover will prevent heat loss by evaporation.

There are several types of solar collectors on the market that can be used to heat pools. Solar pool heaters provide large quantities of warm water, not small quantities of hot water. Because high temperatures are not required, the water leaving the collector should be only about 10 degrees warmer than when it entered.

You will need a large, sunny roof or an open area available for mounting a 200 to 700 square foot collector system to fit the size of your home pool. Typically the collector area should be about half the surface area of your pool.

Contractor-installed systems begin around $2000. Consider the amount of energy you use to heat your pool, the price you pay for it, and the length of time that you use the pool. A solar water heating system for your pool may add up to be a good investment.

PHOTOVOLTAIC CELLS

Photovoltaic (PV) cells are remarkable devices that convert sunlight directly into electricty. This happens in a seemingly simple manner — the cells just sit silently in the sun and do it, without any moving parts! But behind this apparent simplicity is extremely complex and sophisiticated technology.

PV cells are used in hundreds of different applications throughout the world. Most of them are situations which conventional electric systems cannot easily reach, such as remote water pumping or radio signalling. The reason that they aren't used more is their high cost. The high cost is due to the complicated manufacturing process that promises to come down in cost as demand — and production — go up.

Although PVs may be cost effective for homes that are not connected to the grid, it will be the turn of the century before you can expect them to be competitive with the electricty you buy. But, then, the year 2000 isn't that far away, is it!

Choosing a System

Once your house is weatherized, how can you decide which of the ideas in this book to apply to your house? To choose a system, study your house with these questions in mind: What is the construction of the house — is it wood frame or masonry? How is the house oriented in relation to the sun? Are there trees or buildings shading the south side of the house in the winter? How many windows are there and in what direction do they face? Does the house never get enough sun or do the windows it currently has already overheat it? Does the house have good cross ventilation or could you make it better? Do you have the necessary space for a solar system on the walls, the roof, or out in the yard?

Because a solar wall application or add-on provides heat during the day, can it be located next to a room that's used during the day? How many alterations would you have to make in your house and how complicated would they be? Is the roof slope appropriate for a solar water heater? Can the house's structure support the weight of thermal mass? Is there room to add thermal mass?

The second element to consider is the cost-effectiveness of the system. As the world's supplies of oil, natural gas, and coal continue to dwindle, energy costs will continue to rise. And as energy prices rise, the systems described here will save you even more money and pay for themselves faster.

Check the cost-effectiveness rating of each system and keep in mind that the simplest ideas are often the most effective.

The third important element of your decision is yourself. Some of the projects here are easy for do-it-yourselfers. Others can require substantial experience in concrete and masonry work, carpentry, glazing installation, electrical wiring, or plumbing. If you think you can build a system but you know it will be a challenge, do you have people nearby that you can turn to for advice? Will you have enough time to build the system? Some of them require a lot of labor. Can you start in time to finish before there's any possible damage from storms or freezing, or should you wait until spring? Do you have all the tools you need? This can be a hidden cost. Do you have enough money to buy all the materials you need before you get started? It can be discouraging to be halfway through a construction project and get held up because a local supplier doesn't have the materials you need.

Go through the ideas in this book again. Evaluate how well each design would fit your house, your skills, and your desires. After you choose a system, see the *Appendix* for more information. This book was designed for homeowners — to offer ideas that can be modified to fit your own house. The following examples show how some of the ideas might be applied to representative houses or other types of structures.

EXAMPLES OF THE IDEAS APPLIED TO SIX HOUSES

This house is off to a good start with its large glassed-in porch. **Outside-mounted insulating shutters,** with reflective foil faces, would increase the daily solar input to the porch. At night they would be closed to hold the heat in. The slope of the porch roof could also be an effective reflector for a **wall-mounted solar collector.** Also added are a **domestic hot water collector** and more windows.

This house is a natural for solar energy with its big south-sloping roof and large south windows. It would be even more appropriate for solar application if that roof were a leaky slate roof in need of repair. It could then be **converted into a collector.** If air ducts could not be run easily between the roof and basement storage, a liquid system might ıen be appropriate. The entrance porch offers the possibility of simple conversion to a **glassed-in porch.**

In view of a typical city street comprised of town houses or offices there is a wide variety of possible alterations. It is not necessary that all buildings use solutions that look the same. The need and budget would determine the solar application most appropriate for the occupants.

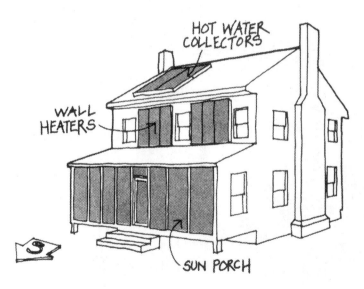

HOT WATER
COLLECTORS

WALL
HEATERS

SUN PORCH

If the porch side of this house faces south, it is a natural for solar energy, with a big south-facing roof and a generous amount of south-facing wall space. Two solar hot water panels have been installed between the windows. Fans blow the hot air through ducts from the panels into second floor rooms. The front porch has been converted into a Sunspace, with glass on the south-facing walls. The closed-in and insulated east and west walls of the porch have windows that can be opened for ventilation. On winter nights, thermal curtains are drawn over all the windows in the house.

With both yard space and wall space available for solar collection, a lean-to collector with rock storage could be used across the entire south face of the building. If the building is masonry, it could be partially converted into vertical wall mounted collectors between the windows. The roof angle is good for a pumped domestic hot water heater and the porch could be enclosed for an entry foyer.

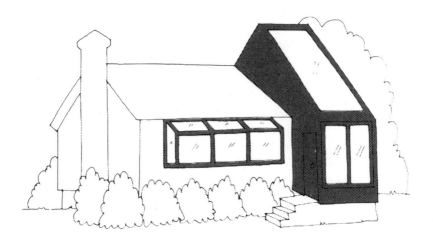

Greenhouse frames around each south-facing window, a new entry foyer and solar domestic hot water structure could be added to this house. Also, additional shrubbery acts as insulation.

Glossary

British thermal unit, or Btu — The quantity of heat needed to raise the temperature of 1 pound of water by 1 degree F.

cellulose — An insulation in construction made from reprocessed paper and other wood by-products.

fiberglass — This insulating material is available in flexible batts and rigid boards and is usually made from a mineral base.

heat exchanger — A device (like a coiled copper tube) that transfers heat from one fluid, such as air or water, to another. A car radiator is an example of a heat exchanger.

heat pump — This is a device which has the ability to take heat from a cold place, thereby making that place colder, and transferring that heat to a warm place, making that place warmer. This is a means of warming a house. This process can be reversed for cooling.

insolation — The amount of solar radiation — direct, diffuse and reflected — striking a surface exposed to the sky.

kilowatt-hour (kWh) — The amount of energy equivalent to one thousand watts of power being used for one hour. This is equivalent of 3413 Btu.

radiant panel heating — These panels have integral passages for the flow of warm air or liquid. Alternatively, they are heated by electrical coils. The warmed panel heats the room by thermal radiation.

R-value — The measure of the ability of a material such as insulation to resist the flow of heat. The higher the R-value, the better the insulation.

retrofit — re-fitting an existing building with solar heating or cooling.

thermal mass — Different contruction materials store heat for varying lengths of time. Heavy materials like concrete, masonry, and water provide thermal mass for a house. These materials store heat and allow the house to remain in a comfortable temperature range while the temperature outside fluctuates.

thermosiphoning — The natural movement of warmed fluids such as water and air. Cool fluids are denser than warm fluids and drop because of gravity. Warm fluids are lighter; they rise and carry heat upwards.

ureaformaldehyde — A foamed-in-place insulation that can no longer be used because of its adverse health effects.

Appendix

The books and publications listed here are both current and out-of-print. Many are still available from the publisher or your local bookstore, but many can only be found at your library or through inter-library loan. New books about energy are coming out all the time, so check your local library for an up-to-date list.

BOOKS:

Ametek Inc. *Solar Energy Handbook*. Radnor, PA: Chilton Book Co., 1983. Solar theory and applications.

Anderson, Bruce, ed. *Ecoloque. The Environmental Catalogue and Consumer's Guide for a Safe Earth*. New York, NY: Prentice-Hall Press, 1990. How to make your buying habits and your lifestyle benefit the environment.

Anderson, Bruce, with Michael Riordan. *The New Solar Home Book*. Acton, MA: Brick House Publishing Co., Inc. 1987. The Smithsonian calls it the "best book to date on solar energy...easy to read format, illustrations and style of writing make this book as attractive as its content."

Clegg, P., and D. Watkins. *The Complete Greenhouse Book*. Pownal, VT: Garden Way Publishing, 1978. Building and using greenhouses from cold frames to solar structures. Information on horticulture, solar, conservation.

Cole, John N., and Charles Wing. *From the Ground Up: The Shelter Institute Guide to Building Your Own House*. Boston, MA: Atlantic Little, Brown & Co., 1976. A complete illustrated guide to owner building.

Eccli, Eugene, ed. *Low-Cost Energy Efficient Shelter for the Owner and Builder*. Emmaus, PA: Rodale Press, Inc., 1976. Excellent treatment of a broad range of energy conserving ideas for the home.

Fisher, Rick and W. Yanda. *The Food and Heat Producing Solar Greenhouse: Design, Construction, Operation*. Santa Fe, NM: John Muir Publications, 1976. Charts, photos, and diagrams

Franklin Research Center. *Installation Guidelines for Solar Domestic Hot Water Systems in One and Two Family Dwellings*. Washington, DC: Superintendent of Documents, U.S. Printing Office, 1979. For the professional contractor and skilled homeowner.

Gay, Larry. *The Complete Book of Insulating*. Brattleboro, VT: The Stephen Green Press, 1980. A complete reference to the theory, materials, and techniques of insulating.

Hardenbrook, Harry. *The Insulator's Estimating Handbook*. Chicago, IL: Frank R. Walker Co., 1980. A full discussion on building insulating practices.

Kern, Ken. *The Owner-Built Home*. Oakhurst, CA: Owner Builder Publications, Sierra Route, 1961. Innovative approach to home construction and design, with good sensible ideas.

Langdon, Bill. *Movable Insulation*. Emmaus, PA: Rodale Press, Inc., 1980. A guide to reducing window heat losses in your home.

Levy, M. Emanuel, Deane Evans, and Cynthia Gardstein. *Passive Solar Construction Handbook*. Emmaus, PA: Rodale Press, 1983. Details and theory behind building for passive solar energy utilization.

Mazria, Edward. *The Passive Solar Energy Book*. Emmaus, PA: Rodale Press, Inc., 1979. Fundamental concepts of passive design and application: numbers, mathematical equations, in simplified form, with illustrations and photos.

McCullagh, James. *The Solar Greenhouse Book*. Emmaus, PA: Rodale Press, Inc., 1978. Complete discussion on design, construction, and operation of solar greenhouses.

Moffit, Anne, and Marc Shiler. *Landscape Design That Saves Energy*. New York, NY: William Morrow & Co., Inc, 1981. Reducing residential energy requirements by up to 30 percent in cool, hot-arid, and hot-humid climates.

NCAT. *Energy-Efficient Home Construction: Basic Superinsulation Techniques*. Butte, MT: National Center for Appropriate Technology, 1984.

NCAT. *Greenhouses: Suggested Reading Lists.*Butte, MT: National Center for Appropriate Technology, 1990.

NCAT. *Low-Cost Passive Solar Greenhouses*. Butte, MT: National Center for Appropriate Technology, 1981.

NCAT. *NCAT Energy Conservation and Renewable Energy Bibliograpy. Butte, MT: National Center for Appropriate Technology, 1990.*

NCAT. *Solar Energy: Suggested Readings*. Butte, MT: National Center for Appropriate Technology, 1990.

NCAT. *Weatherstripping vs. Caulking...And How to Choose the Right Materials to Stop Air Leaks*. Butte, MT: National Center for Appropriate Technology, 1980..

NCAT. *Window Insulation: How to Sort Through the Options*. Butte, MT: National Center for Appropriate Technology, 1984..

NYSERDA. *Making Your Own Solar Hot Water.* Albany, NY: New York State Energy Research and Development Authority, 1982. Complete instructions and blueprints.

NYSERDA. *Making Your Own Solar Structures.* Albany, NY: New York State Energy Research and Development Authority, 1982. Complete instructions and blueprints.

NYSERDA. *Making Your Own Solar Wall Panel.* Albany, NY: New York State Energy Research and Development Authority, 1982. Complete instructions and blueprints.

Paige, Stephen. *Solar Water Heating for the Handyman.* Barrington, NJ: Edmund Scientific Co., 1974. For the handy-person.

Portola Institute. *Energy Primer.* Menlo Park, CA: Portola Institute, 1978. A solid introduction to solar and other energy sources.

Reif, Daniel R. *Passive Solar Water Heaters.* Andover, MA: Brick House Publishing Co., 1983. How to design and build a batch solar water heating system.

Reif, Daniel R. *Solar Retrofit.* Andover, MA: Brick House Publishing Co., 1981. Adding solar to your home: how to build four solar heating systems.

Shurcliff, William A. *Thermal Shutters and Shades.* Andover, MA: Brick House Publishing Co., Inc., 1980. From basic heat loss concepts, to shutter and shade design, and the pros and cons of different materials, with over 700 drawings and diagrams.

Shapiro, Andrew. *Complete Handbook for Add-On Solar Greenhouses & Sunspaces.* Emmaus, PA: Rodale Press. 1985. Planning, design and construction of attached solar greenhouses and sunspaces for solar heating, horticulture, or solarium use.

Temple, Peter L. and Jennifer A. Adams. *Solar Heating. A Construction Manual.* Radnor, PA: Chilton Book Co., 1981. Site-built roof and wall air panels for the experienced do-it-yourselfer.

Twitchell, Mary. *Solar Projects for Under $500.* Pownal, VT: Storey Communications, Inc., 1985. Eighteen practical designs for energy efficiency.

Wilson, Tom, ed. *Home Remedies: A Guidebook for Residential Retrofit.* Philadelphia, PA: Mid-Atlantic Solar Energy Association. Guidelines for accomplishing a retrofit analyzing, doing it, getting help. Includes Trombe wall, greenhouses, hot water.

Wolfe, Delores E. *Growing Food in Solar Greenhouses*. New York, NY: Doubleday, 1981. Month-to-month guide to growing vegetables, fruits, and herbs under glass. Also resources, suppliers, seeds, books, and natural pest control.

PUBLICATIONS (PAST AND PRESENT):

Although many of these magazines are out of print, they may still be available at your library. They contain a great wealth of solar information.

Energy Auditor and Retrofitter

Home Energy

Home Resource

New Shelter

Northeast Sun

Popular Science

Solar Age Magazine

Solar Energy

Solar Today

HOW-TO-DO-IT PLANS

Contact these organizations for plans for the do-it-yourself market.

Brace Research Institute. *How to Build a Solar Water Heater*. Ask for Do-it-yourself Leaflet No. L–4. McGill University, Montreal, Province of Quebec, Canada.

Domestic Technology Institute. *Attached Greenhouse Plans*. From the Institute at Box 2043, Evergreen, CO 80439. (303) 674-1597

Environmental Information Center of the Florida Conservation Foundation, Inc. *Build Your Own Solar Water Heater*. From the Center at 1251B Miller Ave., Winter Park, FL 32789 (407) 644-5377.

Solstice Publications. *Attached Greenhouse Movable Insulation System and Domestic Hot Water System Plans*. A brochure lists the many blueprints available and their costs. Solstice Publication, Box 2043, Evergreen, CO 80439. (303) 674-1597

Zomeworks Corporation. *Solar Water Heater Plans*. P.O. Box 25805, Albuquerque, NM 87125 (505) 242-5354

Zomeworks Corporation. *Breadbox Water Heater Plans*. P.O. Box 25805, Albuquerque, NM 87125 (505) 242-5354

ORGANIZATIONS:

There are many organizations around the country that promote energy conservation and the use of renewable energies. Check with your State offices for a Governor's Energy Council and the American Solar Energy Society for state, regional, or private organizations nearest you.

American Council for an Energy-Efficient Economy
1001 Connecticut Avenue NW, Suite 535, Washington, DC 20036
(202)429-8873. (202) 429-8873

American Solar Energy Society, Inc. United States Section of the International Solar Energy Society (ASES)
2400 Central Ave. Unit B–l, Boulder, CO 80301. (303) 443–3130.
National and international information on conservation and renewables.

Chapters:

Alabama Solar Energy Association
c/o UAH/ASEC, Solar Test Facility, Huntsville, AL 35899

Arizona Solar Energy Association
PO Box 1886, Chino Valley, AZ 86323, (602) 636-2765

Florida Solar Energy Association
2519 N. Ocean Blvd., Apt. 512A, Boca Raton, FL 33431

Illinois Solar Energy Association
1361 Westchester, Glendale Heights, IL 60139, (312) 690-3975

Kansas Solar Energy Society
1602 So. McLean, Witchita, KS 67217

Minnesota Solar Energy Association
PO Box 762, Minneapolis, MN 55440, (612) 298-1001

Mississippi Solar Energy Association
225 West Lumpkin Road, Starkville, MS 39759, (601) 323-7246

Nevada Solar Advocates
Truckee Meadows Community College, 7000 Dandini Blvd.
Reno, NV 89512

North Carolina Solar Energy Association
850 West Morgan Street, Raleigh, NC 27603, (919) 832-7601

Nebraska Solar Energy Association
University of Nebraska at Omaha, Engineering Building 110
60th and Dodge, Omaha, NE 68182, (402) 554-2669

Northeast Sunstainable Energy Association
23 Ames Street, Greenfield, MA 01301, (413) 774-6051

Northern California Energy Association
PO Box 3008, Berkeley, CA 94703

Ohio Solar Energy Association
Kent State University, School of Architecture, 304 Taylor Hall
Kent, OH 44242, (216) 672-2869

Solar Energy Association of Oregon
2637 SW Water Ave., Portland, OR 97201, (503) 224-7867

Southern California Solar Energy Association
339 20th Street, Santa Monica, CA 90402

Texas Solar Energy Society
PO Box 3682, Austin, TX 78764, (512) 339-8562

Conservation and Renewable Energy Inquiry and Referral Service (CAREIRS)
Box 8900, Silver Spring, MD 20907 (800) 523-2929.
Got a question about energy conservation or alternative energy? They've got the answers — in brochures, factsheets, bibliographies, with referrals to trade associations, researchers, state and local groups, federal agencies, special interest groups, and professional associations. And it's free.

Florida Solar Energy Center (FSEC)
300 State Road 401, Cape Canaveral, FL 32920. (407) 783-0300.
Technical and consumer publications, research and development, standards and training programs.

Mid-Atlantic Solar Energy Association (MASEA)
2233 Gray's Ferry Ave., Philadelphia, PA. A regional chapter of ASES.

National Center for Appropriate Technology (NCAT)
P.O. Box 4000, Butte, MT 59702. (406) 494-4572. See **NATAS**. Helping individuals explore appropriate technologies as solutions to a variety of social problems.

National Appropriate Technology Assistance Service (NATAS)
P.O. Box 2525, Butte, MT 59702. (800) 428-2525. In Montana (800) 428-1718. Advice to implement projects that use energy conservation and renewable energy technologies..

New York State Energy Research and Development Authority (NY-SERDA)
Communications Dept .2, Rockefeller Plaza, Albany, NY 12223. (518) 465-6251.

Passive Solar Industries Council (PSIC)
1090 Vermont Ave.N.W., Suite 1200, Washington DC 20005 (202)371-0357.

Solar Energy Industries Association (SEIA), 777 North Capitol Street, Suite 805 N.E., Washington, DC 20002. (202) 408–0660.

Solar Energy Research Institute (SERI)
1617 Cole Blvd., Golden CO 80401. (303) 231–1415.

PROFESSIONAL ORGANIZATIONS
These groups also promote energy conservation and solar energy.

American Institute of Architects (AIA)
1735 New York Ave., N.W., Washington, DC 20006. (202) 626–7300.

American Society of Heating Refrigeration, and
Air Conditioning Engineers (ASHRAE)
1791 Tullie Circle N.E., Atlanta, GA 30329. (404) 636–8400.

National Association of Home Builders (NAHB)
15th and M Streets, N.W., Washington, DC 20005. (202) 822–0200.

U.S. Department of Energy (USDOE)
1000 Independence Ave., Washington, DC 20585. (202) 252–5000.

NOTES

NOTES